PERILS
&
CONSEQUENCES

PERILS

&

CONSEQUENCES

TO THE AGENT ON BEHALF OF THE CLIENT

RICH VOTAW WITH STAN SCOTT

authorHOUSE®

AuthorHouse™
1663 Liberty Drive
Bloomington, IN 47403
www.authorhouse.com
Phone: 1 (800) 839-8640

Published by AuthorHouse   09/14/2015

ISBN: 978-1-5049-3388-9 (sc)
ISBN: 978-1-5049-3389-6 (hc)
ISBN: 978-1-5049-3387-2 (e)

Library of Congress Control Number: 2015914009

Print information available on the last page.

Any people depicted in stock imagery provided by Thinkstock are models, and such images are being used for illustrative purposes only. Certain stock imagery © Thinkstock.

This book is printed on acid-free paper.

This book is dedicated to two of the wisest men whom I have ever known, Ned Vukovich and Sammy Krzich.

Vechnaya Pamyat…

"Long-term commitment to new learning and new philosophy is required of any management that seeks transformation. The timid and the fainthearted, and the people that expect quick results, are doomed to disappointment."

- W. Edwards Deming

Author's Note

The uncertainty in life is what makes insurance so important. When insurance is applied with the highest ethical standards, it can make an enormous difference on a business, an individual, or a family. Insurance and the transfer of risk are noble pursuits that have contributed to the standard of living that is enjoyed today in this country. The United States would not be the world leader that it is today if not for the health of its insurance industry.

Why then do the insurance industry and the insurance profession have serious public perception issues? Why is it that a humane endeavor of social conscience, as such, is not more revered by the public?

Fifteen years ago, I set off on a journey to determine why people, businesses, and entities need to buy insurance, and how I could add value to that process. I attended seminars, visited successful insurance agencies, and picked up tips from anybody and everybody. I was learning how to do it, but was lacking something: my purpose, my mission, my salvation.

I discovered through my search that there is too much emphasis on the marketing and the price of the insurance at hand, and there are far too many people in the marketplace buying the wrong insurance. Therein, I found the opportunity for success.

It is our responsibility to prepare and educate ourselves so that we are able to assist our clients in their most critical endeavor of having the proper and suitable insurance in place at all times. We must honor and respect every hard-earned dollar they spend or invest under our watch.

These beliefs are all ethical considerations—they are about doing the right thing!

With these beliefs, I developed a clear mission statement—a proclamation of what my business does and its purpose in people's lives. It is a well though-out, comprehensive, and significant promise that holds me accountable to my clients. It sets me apart and gives me a unique edge over my competitors.

Along with the mission statement comes a declaration of intent—a unique selling proposition composed of six principles. I use these principles in all of my business transactions.

The mission statement and declaration of intent have freed me from the confines of an industry that places too much emphasis on the price of insurance and the marketing of insurance. The vision that I am about to share with you will enable you to exploit the unlimited opportunity that awaits you in the insurance marketplace. My purpose is to provide you with the knowledge needed to assist your clients in transferring the insurmountable risk that they face every day.

Perils and Consequences is designed to restore honor to our profession, the type of honor that treats your client as they were your family, the type of honor that respects every hard-earned dollar your clients give to you and the type of honor that causes you to study your profession on a constant basis.

This book is written as a story about a conversation between three insurance agents. This story will explain a defined mission and purpose relating to insurance sales. This mission is based on logic, rationale and mathematics. The lessons contained in this book will teach you how to transform the logic, rationale and mathematics into a coherent and concise verbal presentation. You will learn that the adherence to sound principles will transform your business life and the lives of your clients.

"Vision without action is a daydream. Action without vision is a nightmare."

- Japanese Proverb

THE DECLARATION OF INTENT

Tony sits rocking with the motion of the car, nervously counting down the hours until the two-day insurance conference. This is his first conference since he joined the business a few months ago, and he hopes that he will finally learn what it takes to be an effective insurance broker.

Glancing over at Tony's eager face, Darko smirks. He thinks back to the beginning of his career. Surely he was just as excited as Tony to be involved in the protecting and insuring of others. He turns toward the window searching for a glimmer of excitement within, but loses interest and turns his attention to the changing landscape.

Ned adjusts his rear view mirror to glimpse at the faces of his two colleagues. To him, it seems a looking glass. Tony, he thinks, is receptive and eager to grow. He smiles at this thought, and then turns a concerned eye toward Darko, who seems distant and removed.

Tony has just made a huge life change, resulting from the dissatisfaction and disillusionment he was feeling on a daily basis. Working ten-hour days as a banker at one of the nation's premier financial institutions, Tony was uninspired and unappreciated by his boss and coworkers. Six months ago, when he could no longer take it, he left his monetarily secure position to take up an insurance brokerage. He had always wanted to run his own business, and starting an insurance brokerage was a great way to start. Ever since he left the bank, though, his wife has been worried, anxious and constantly reminding him of the uncertainty that lies ahead. He is optimistic that this car ride with Ned—his mentor—and the conference, will finally lead to the confidence he needs to reassure his wife—and himself—that his choice was the right one.

Darko, on the other hand, has been an insurance broker for nearly a decade. He has known Ned through working in the same field and attending conferences together. While Ned is viewed as one of his agency's top brokers, Darko has not enjoyed his job or felt competent in the field of risk management since he first began eight years ago. Every day in the office for him is a negative blur—*policies, policies, policies* running through his mind. Darko is aware of the success Ned has encountered over his lengthy career, but has never sought out any of his advice.

Tony and Darko graciously requested that Ned accompany them to the conference. A 20-year veteran of the business, he knows from first-hand experience what each of these apprentices are currently experiencing day-to-day. He has come properly equipped with materials and references to show them the way toward a happier life. Reaching over to the seat beside him, he picks up one of many resources he intends to share with these two. Breaking the silence, he hands the paper back in Tony's direction and says, "Read and recite, please."

Tony glances over at Darko, who looks disinterested, and clears his throat to read the first sentence on the page aloud. **"Our mission is to safeguard our clients against financial ruin,"** he says.

Darko's ears perk up, and Ned asks Tony to continue reading.

"This mission is accomplished by following these six principles:

1. At our agency we handle most, or all, of our client's insurance and act as their insurance advisor.
2. We help them develop an insurance buying strategy tailored to their individual needs and provide them the needed protection in the event of a worst-case scenario.
3. We bring to our client's attention the financial exposures they have regarding the four insurance perils: *property insurance, lawsuit exposure, medical insurance and loss of income.*

4. We find that most people are over-insured where coverage is least needed and under-insured where coverage is most needed.
5. We diagnose their exposure to the four financial perils and then help them obtain suitable coverage
6. We conduct a face to face meeting with our clients and prospects to ensure our mission is accomplished."

"Thank you for reading both our **mission statement** and our **declaration of intent**, Tony," Ned says. "You are a wonderful orator."

"That sure is a mouthful," Darko says, "Do you recite the whole thing daily?"

"Darko, I have never known you to be at a loss for words," Ned kids, "so, if you start using my mission statement, at least then you'll be able to ensure that you are always talking about something substantial. Maybe you'll find this to be a pleasant detour from your past."

"Yeah, yeah, go ahead, belittle me again," Darko counters.

Since they are old friends, Ned and Darko often engage in this type of playful, yet sarcastic, banter.

"Darko, although I may not say it word for word, and in fact it varies from time to time, I am sure to utilize these principles in all my activities and business transactions," Ned says.

"Sounds a bit lofty," Darko remarks.

"It is, and should be, lofty," Ned says, "After all, insurance is your client's financial foundation,"

"My mission statement and declaration of intent are proclamations of what my business does and its purpose in people's lives," he continues. "This pledge is unique from my competition and gives me a great advantage. It makes me accountable to my clients and allows me to stand out from my competition. It is a well-thought-out, comprehensive, and significant promise."

"I have read about what mission statements are and how important they can be," Tony adds.

"A mission statement is not just important," Ned starts, "it is absolutely essential to your business life. It sets you apart and gives you a unique edge over your competitor. It also shows people why they should choose you for their specific needs."

Tony reflects on this for a moment.

Ned continues, "Your mission statement should briefly and clearly state what it is that you do for your clients. It gives you a unique selling proposition."

"I bet most business people couldn't even say what sets them apart from people doing the same business," Tony interjects.

"You are so right, Tony," Ned says. "Most people don't give much thought to their uniqueness in the market. They assume being a part of it is enough, but this notion is lazy and unwise.

"Knowing what you are proposing to do for your client, or having a mission, helps set you apart from those who have no idea where they are trying to go. Most importantly, a mission statement is not just something you say, it is everything you do, all the time."

With much more clarity, Tony realizes, "So, having a mission statement, or a unique selling proposition, gives you direction, not only in business, but in life."

Ned nods.

"Along with this mission statement, I have developed my own declaration of intent.

"I am hoping that, over the next few days, I can provide you with a compass to travel in new directions on a bold journey. I want to present to you a fresh and groundbreaking approach to personal insurance sales that our agency has already implemented into its daily operations."

"Revolution through a few statements and principles sounds too good to be true," Darko remarks.

"Darko, I promise, the principles are just the tools you have been searching for," Ned says. "Over the next few days, I will break down all six of them and show you how they are integral to the fulfilling of our mission statement. Not only will I show you **how** to do it but, more importantly to me, **why** you should. That is my purpose, my mission, my sincere intent," he finishes.

"Man, you get so deep you scare me," Darko says, sitting up straighter, and then continuing, "This seems like an intense approach to insurance but, from past experience, I've come to understand and respect that your overall philosophy is very solid.

"I think in the past I've always been too busy to change, but lately I've been realizing I'm performing like a hamster on a treadmill. All the while *policy, policy, policy* has been raging through my brain.

"I've seen the considerable amount of personal freedom you enjoy and understand that it hasn't been handed to you. I've watched you read, plan and budget. I've heard you speak on almost every topic relating to our business. In short, I am with you for these next few days so I can get off the treadmill that dominates my life," Darko finishes.

"So, are you ready to incorporate a mission statement into your operations?" Ned asks. "Is it true that I have convinced you that it is ludicrous to operate without a clear and defined purpose?"

Both Tony and Darko nod their heads in agreement.

"Most people in the work force don't know how to manage themselves because, in the past, they were told what to do," Ned says.

"With a mission statement and a declaration of intent, you will learn to manage yourself instead of floating aimlessly along, always wondering what it is you need to do to succeed."

With unbridled enthusiasm, Tony says, "I am definitely on board for the duration of this lesson."

"Excellent, Tony," Ned says. "Our declaration of intent requires all participants to be on board. Over the next few days, you'll come to understand that the principles of the declaration of intent have to be utilized in all operations, at all times, by all staff—not just one individual. Quite frankly, these are the rules of the game, compromising any of the principles is unacceptable.

"After all, my declaration of intent is designed to assist your clients in the purchasing of the right insurance in order to protect their income and assets for years to come," Ned says. "And protecting your clients with the right insurance should always be your goal.

"Allow me to provide you with an outline of our discussion, directed by the declaration of intent.

- First, we need to discuss why you should approach insurance as a trusted advisor and how to view insurance as one product with one solution.
- Next, we will discuss the implementation of an expert insurance buying strategy that focuses on the avoidance of financial ruin.
- Then, we will discuss the four financial perils all consumers face today.
- After you understand the four financial perils, I will then explain the realities of consequential and inconsequential insurance coverage.
- I will then teach you how to diagnose a client's exposure to the four financial perils and subsequently assist them in placing the suitable coverage for all of their consequential exposures.
- Finally, we will discuss conducting a personal comprehensive insurance review."

"There sure is a lot of information there," Tony says a bit skeptically, "I hope that as you break it down it will become easier to understand than it is now as a whole."

"It will," Ned reassures him. "By demonstrating the practical and comprehensive insurance review, one that builds trust and respect from your clients, you will be able to become risk managers—trusted insurance advisors who clearly and concisely communicate to the client based on the mission statement and declaration of intent.

"Improved communication is imperative and will help you explain why insurance will protect your clients' assets and income against financial ruin," Ned stresses. "You will be able to help them build a personal financial foundation with an irrefutable solution to future loss."

"Then you believe an agent cannot become a trusted insurance advisor without implementing a clear and concise mission statement?" Tony says.

"Exactly," Ned says. "You can't become a trusted advisor if you don't know what you are doing. If you don't have a mission statement or directive you can only know what you are doing some of the time. A golf pro once told me that if you don't have a target, then your target is everywhere."

"It does sound as though your mission statement takes the selling out of the process," Darko interjects. "And people don't like to be sold."

Ned smiles realizing that a shift has already begun, "Perfect, Darko. People do not want to be sold; they want to be told.

"They want to be spoken to directly about their insurance. When you speak directly to them about the possibility of losing all their hard-earned assets and future income as a result of being under-insured, they will openly tell you their annual income and net worth. Then, you can use that information to help them purchase suitable insurance. They will want to protect what they have and will willingly follow your advice.

"The more you approach insurance this way, the more you will find that most people you encounter in the marketplace are either grossly under-insured in a critical area or lack an insurance buying strategy. Sometimes it is the wrong liability limits, too low of deductibles, the wrong medical plan, or no life insurance. There will almost always be some deficiency in all of your prospects' insurance programs.

"Most often, after demonstrating the insufficiency in their insurance program, I am able to secure them as a client for life because they know and believe I am looking out for their best interests," Ned completes his thought.

"When you say most people in the marketplace are either grossly under-insured or lack an insurance buying strategy, what percentage of the market would you consider this to be?" Darko inquires.

"Darko, it is at least 95 percent," Ned says. "Using the principles of my declaration of intent you will begin to uncover these deficiencies. I advocate that you focus your efforts on identifying your clients' risks. I believe that the standards that bind insurance agents are far too low. These standards must be raised in order to resurrect the reputation of our profession.

"Ignoring a person's financial condition or situation and still selling them an insurance policy should be viewed as reckless and irresponsible," Ned adds.

"I have given this discussion much thought and want you to understand that some of my ideas and beliefs may be threatening and even uncomfortably challenge you. But my understanding is that you both have the desire and need to be mentored. I ask that you open both your hearts and minds and, let's all agree, be as candid as possible with one another. Are we in agreement?"

Both men nod their heads.

"I'm ready to make the choice. I will adopt your mission statement," Darko says, his pessimism fading.

"Will you also adopt the mission of driving?" Ned asks, already handing Darko the keys.

The men smile at each other and Darko willingly takes the keys, suggesting they stretch their legs before switching spots. Everyone agrees.

Chapter 1 Summary

- To succeed in any business, you must have a mission statement that sets you apart from your competitors, explains your purpose and shows customers/clients why you are the most capable of meeting their needs.
- Having a clear, concise mission statement is vital and should reflect in all business transactions.
- A mission statement should be carried out through a set of principles—or declaration of intent—that guides all employees to self-management and accountability.
- An example of a well-thought-out and successful mission statement for an insurance agency is: **Our mission is to safeguard our clients against financial ruin**.
- An example of a declaration of intent to follow this mission statement is:

1. **At our agency we handle most, or all, of our client's insurance and act as their insurance advisor.**
2. **We help them develop an insurance buying strategy tailored to their individual needs and provide them the needed protection in the event of a worst-case scenario.**
3. **We bring to our client's attention the financial exposures they have regarding the four insurance perils:** *property insurance, lawsuit exposure, medical insurance and loss of income.*
4. **We find that most people are over-insured where coverage is least needed and under-insured where coverage is most needed.**
5. **We diagnose their exposure to the four financial perils and then help them obtain suitable coverage.**
6. **We conduct a face to face meeting with our clients and prospects to ensure our mission is accomplished.**

"There is no human problem which could not be solved if people would simply do as I advise."

- Gore Vidal

CHAPTER 2

GUIDING THE WAY AS ADVISOR

"Darko, Tony, now that I've introduced my mission statement and declaration of intent, let's begin our discussion in detail. Any objections?" Ned asks as they all return to the car.

Darko is now in the driver's seat and settles in and grabs the seatbelt behind him being sure to take the opportunity to poke some fun at Ned, "I guess I'm ready—my seatbelt is buckled."

"You better be, you funny guy," Ned counters and then says, "The first principle of my declaration of intent is, once again,

At our agency we handle most or all of our client's insurance and act as their insurance advisor.

"What does this position say to you, Tony?" Ned asks the junior devotee.

"Well, handling all of someone's insurance gives them the one-stop-shopping advantage," Tony answers.

"Hmmm, interesting answer, however, it is also predictable," Ned says. "I am certain you'll find this ride, as well as my responses, to be unpredictable."

He then continues with this explanation, "First of all, I don't concur with the one-stop-shopping advantage because there is no advantage to one-stop-shopping if you end up buying the wrong insurance."

10

"Good point, Ned, I never looked at it from that perspective," Darko says.

Tony, in an attempt to save face, counters, "Well, then, it *is* an advantage if the client ends up with the *right* insurance."

"I suppose, but I don't like the implication of this statement," Ned continues. "One-stop-shopping implies that you are shopping, a word better suited to describe the purchasing of tangible consumer products. The problem is that insurance is an intangible financial shield designed to transfer financial risk. So, purchasing insurance requires a sound strategy based on a concise philosophy. You shouldn't shop for this type of protection," Ned finishes.

"Point taken, I guess you don't go shopping for stocks and investments either," Tony rebounds.

"Exactly, financial products are too important to trivialize with words like shopping," says Ned. "Remember, words and expressions are powerful and have great implications, so, please, strike the 'one-stop-shopping' phrase from your vernacular."

"Aye, aye, captain," Darko chuckles.

"Good, now let's get back to our core discussion," Ned says.

"*At our agency we handle most or all of our client's insurance and act as their insurance advisor.* The main objective for my agency is to be an advisor to our entire clientele."

"That's a broad statement, Ned," Darko interjects.

"Broad, yet definitive, Darko," Ned says. "Insurance is undeniably the unequivocal financial foundation for all of our clients. This reality gives us no other choice than to advise them.

"I am not a salesperson. I am an advisor. Insurance has too great of consequences to simply be sold. Salespeople confuse. People relent to their pushy arrogance, but concur with direct and personal advisors. Salespeople are adversaries who offer no solutions. Advisors are coaches who eliminate choices and offer irrefutable solutions. Customers recognize the difference between salespeople and advisors. People are skeptical of salespeople but walk hand in hand with advisors who act in their best interests," Ned concludes.

"Wow," Darko says. "Sounds great, but it seems a bit daunting to me."

"Daunting now, but I believe it will eventually be attainable even for you, Darko," Ned jabs.

"There is urgency, more than ever, for our profession to transition from selling to advising. Far too often in the past, insurance has been sold without regard to its potential consequence. This phenomenon has had damaging effects on our collective reputation and needs mending," Ned finishes.

"Interesting, don't you think, Tony?" Darko says. "I'm sure we are going to find that we have been selling, rather than advising, more than we think."

"I am certain we will," Tony responds.

"My intent is to distinguish selling from advising and advance each of you further down the road to becoming a trusted insurance advisor," Ned says.

"It is the only logical approach and it is imperative that you understand and embrace *why* this is the case," Ned says.

"Once I receive your commitment, we can then progress to *how* I accomplish this with my customers. Being an advisor and utilizing my comprehensive mission statement will help you attain preeminence in the field.

"You will learn that putting your clients' best interests before your own will lead to success. When businesses fail to understand their clients' needs and address them before they address the needs of the company, they become unremarkable and unmemorable."

Darko interrupts Ned and says, "I guess I'm unremarkable and unmemorable when it's put this way. That really hurts."

"Darko, you've had considerable success. Unremarkable and unmemorable are descriptions I believe you can overcome," Ned clarifies.

"Insurance people get caught up in the wrong things. They are worried about their signs, symbols, and sales," Ned says. "Instead, they should be concerned most about the client."

Ned adds, "With this said, proving to be a trusted insurance advisor is your expression of love to your clients, managers, sales reps, and even your underwriters."

"Love your underwriters? Now that's a tall order," Darko says.

"I have some excellent underwriters who I really like," Tony says.

"As a trusted advisor you will come to love them because, coming from this position, you will earn their respect," Ned says. "They will quickly come to understand and recognize that your intent is honorable, and they will work with you to place the business that you present to them."

"Could you expand on that thought?" Darko says.

"Don't worry, Darko. I understand that you will always need more explaining than Tony. I have prepared myself for that reality," Ned pokes at Darko before continuing.

"It is commonplace to deliver customer service in your job. You're supposed to return phone calls, print evidences of insurance, and complete all your unskilled tasks for your clients. These are things that will not set you apart."

"That makes sense, but it is amazing that so many of my competitors don't get back to their clients," Tony says. "In fact, that's how I get a lot of my clients. I think doing this leads to excellent customer satisfaction."

"The truth is that your customers are only satisfied because they have not suffered a catastrophic loss," Ned says. "The question is, will your clients still be satisfied if they end up losing everything because they bought the wrong insurance?

"Having satisfied customers isn't good enough anymore. If you really want to build your agency, you have to create genuinely loyal clients who understand that your advice supersedes all other factors and is paramount to their insurance portfolio," he states.

"Boy, you really keep rocking our paradigms," Darko says.

"Yeah, you can say that again," Tony agrees. "I've been boasting about all the wrong things. I get your point on customer satisfaction."

"Truth be told, I think the whole concept of customer satisfaction has no value concerning insurance," Ned says, adding, "Satisfaction is not an acceptable standard of customer service in my agency. The standard and measure of success in my agency is a loyal client—a client who has all their business under our watch. In addition, they will have purchased the right insurance and look at us as their trusted insurance advisors. Protecting them is our way of expressing love for our clients."

"I think we get this," Tony says and then jumps ahead, "What do you mean when you describe insurance as a single product?"

"Excellent question, Tony," Ned praises. "In fact, that's the next concept I was about to communicate. The **single product theory** means that when selling personal insurance to a family or individual you look at it as one single product made up of numerous components. These components—policies and conditions—are purchased for the sole purpose of transferring risk and providing protection against financial ruin."

"So, what you're saying is that whether you need multiple policies, for example auto, home, or life, you must consider them as one," Tony helps to simplify Ned's thoughts.

"Exactly," Ned says. "For example, take my family. We have two auto policies, a homeowner's, a boat owner's policy, an umbrella policy, and multiple life policies. To look at every policy on its own is overwhelming, but when I look at it from the perspective that I buy all these policies for the sole purpose of safeguarding against financial ruin, it makes the whole thing seem more manageable and easier to comprehend."

"Please consider this: no matter how many policies a client has, what type of coverage they need, or how much your client pays, they are buying it for the singular purpose of transferring their financial risk and safeguarding themselves against financial ruin. It is a single, solitary endeavor. **One product, one advisor, one solution**," Ned finishes.

"That makes perfect sense," Tony says.

"I am glad you agree," Ned says and then expands deeper into his single product theory.

"If we agree that buying all insurance should be a singular endeavor, then we have wholly accepted the premise that insurance has been designed for the sole and singular purpose of transferring the risk of an individual or family. With this belief, I then accept the responsibility of managing all the personal insurance risk of my client.

"This enables me to explain a client's exposures in a seamless, singular presentation. As we go further into our discussion, I will present to you some additional realities that will make clear to you how my associates and I are able to deliver this type of comprehensive insurance presentation," Ned concludes.

"A single product? I like this premise," Darko says, "but how do you explain this to the client?"

"I tell clients that they must look at their entire insurance portfolio as one product made up of multiple policies designed to transfer their financial risk. I further explain that viewing insurance this way will help them avoid gaps in their coverage, as well as eliminate a lack of insurance in any critical area."

"You definitely reduce the chance for gaps and underinsuring by looking at all their coverage at once," Tony adds.

"I believe people need only one risk manager," Ned says. "Having your insurance spread out with two or three agencies can be perilous to one's financial future. Insurance is your client's financial foundation and when I discuss insurance with people I discuss insurance as one product with the many components of auto policies, home policies, health and life policies. I tell them that I am to be viewed as their risk manager and trusted insurance advisor," Ned pauses and then finishes, "One product, one advisor, one solution."

"Sounds great," says Tony. "I hope I'll be able to start selling in this manner."

"You will, Tony. It just takes more education and discipline on your part."

Ned then reviews their discussion of the first principle in his declaration of intent.

At our agency we handle most or all of our client's insurance and act as their insurance advisor.

"In a nutshell, this statement tells my clients that I will handle their insurance as a single product and act as their advisor; I am someone who will act in their best interest at all times."

"What do you mean when you say most or all of their insurance?" Darko asks.

"What I mean by that is there are circumstances when my client isn't able to place all of their personal insurance within our agency. Perhaps they have medical insurance benefits at their work, they may own property in another state where I am not licensed, or they own a property that I don't have a market for. But, even in these cases, I will act as an advisor to my insured," Ned answers.

"So, you will review policies not with your agency?" Darko asks.

"Yes. For example, I may sit down with a customer to help them pick out a health plan offered at work, or check on the reconstruction costs of an out-of-state rental they may own," Ned answers and continues.

"This helps set me apart from all other agents and makes me unique from other professionals. My goal is to be the most competent and trusted of all the professionals my clients will encounter in the marketplace."

"Seems like a lot of extra work to me," Darko says.

"You can't quantify the value you create when you advise without regard to your compensation," Ned says. "This sends a powerful message to your clients and helps demonstrate your significant integrity. It is a standard of excellence."

"I consider this excellence to be lofty, yet attainable," Darko, who is beginning to understand with greater clarity, offers. He sees the value that their association with Ned will bring to their careers.

Tony nods in agreement and turns to look out the window and contemplate this discussion about the declaration of intent's first part. He hones in on the word "advisor" and feels the enormity of the responsibility they have to their clients.

Both men look to Ned and it is clear that they have already subconsciously joined Ned's crusade. Their faces glow with anticipation as they both consider that the best is still yet to come.

Chapter 2 Summary

- In this chapter, we focus on the first principle of the declaration of intent: ***At our agency we handle most or all of our client's insurance and act as their insurance advisor.***
- Because insurance is an intangible financial shield designed to transfer financial risk, it should not be sold.
- Agents must advise their clients on how to purchase all of their insurance using a sound strategy—one that will protect them from financial ruin.
- If you really want to build your agency, you have to create loyal clients who understand that your advice supersedes all other factors and is paramount to their insurance portfolio.
- The standard and measure of success in your agency is a loyal client, one who has all their business under your watch.
- Putting a client's needs in front of your own will ensure your success
- People need only one risk manager; having one's insurance spread out with two or three agencies can be perilous to one's financial future. Thus, the single product theory: ***one product, one advisor, one solution.***

CHAPTER 3

WORST CASE SCENARIO

Darko and Tony, still contemplating the enormity of advising and helping customers with all areas of insurance, turn to Ned and await the next nugget of truth he will provide.

Ned directs Tony to read the second principle in the declaration of intent.

We help [our clients] develop an insurance buying strategy tailored to their individual needs and provide them the needed protection in the event of a worst-case scenario.

"This statement clarifies and defines what I believe a trusted insurance advisor should provide. It tells your client that, with your expertise, you will help them develop an insurance buying strategy for the long haul," Ned says.

"I'm a little apprehensive to call myself an expert since I have so little experience," Tony admits.

"Tony, you're a smart individual," Ned assures him.

"In our past discussions, you've shown me a comprehensive understanding of the policies offered and their conditions. I believe expertise is achieved by adopting and practicing a sound insurance buying strategy based on a common sense philosophy," he says.

"So, by taking the knowledge that I have and then fusing it with your philosophy, I can become an expert?" Tony asks.

"Exactly," Ned says.

"After going through the entire mission statement and philosophy, you'll find that these beliefs and convictions supersede knowledge of the policies and conditions. In short, the implementation of a sound insurance buying strategy will make you an expert," he explains.

He continues, "Expert is defined as 'having much training and knowledge in some special field.' Without both of these things, an agent has no value or purpose."

"You're an advisor. You're an expert. What next? Are you going to tell us you're a Renaissance man?" Darko chides Ned.

"No, Darko," Ned replies. "I am not a Renaissance man. I am simply a mild-mannered, personal lines insurance guy with a defined mission and purpose,"

He then returns to his lecture on the virtues of expertise.

"If you are not an expert advisor, then the only game available to you is the 'Best Price Insurance Game'," he says. "Playing this game makes you an insurance retailer, which we must avoid at all costs.

"Retailing insurance is arduous work. Clients offer you no respect, you command none, and you deserve none because to sell insurance as if it were a consumer product marginalizes our entire industry," Ned continues.

"You must eliminate the discussion of rating factors, discounts, and all of the inconsequential stuff that gets in the way of providing people with the right insurance. If you want to be a respected professional, a difference maker, you have to do more than just sell insurance. You need to provide expertise that enables people to understand why they need to buy insurance."

Ned stops to let Darko interject, "I notice that insurance is almost always marketed on the premise of saving people money."

"Precisely, Darko. You hear it all the time. Marketing strategies such as 'Call me to save money on your insurance', 'Fifteen minutes or less could save you 15 percent or more', 'Good driver discount,' or 'We offer discounts if you have your home and auto insurance with us', proliferate ads in the Yellow Pages, on the television, radio and the Internet. Save, save, save. Discounts, discounts, discounts. It is the prevailing way of marketing insurance.

"Tell me this, how do you save money when you're spending thousands of dollars a year on insurance? Saving money is putting money into your bank or stock investments on a monthly basis. You never, ever, ever save money on insurance. You will only spend money on insurance," Ned stops to catch his breath.

Tony offers, "Even in my short time in the business, I've already heard many times the adage: sell on price, lose on price."

"Good, Tony. I believe your purpose is to be an expert risk manager to all of your clients," Ned says. "The 'Best Price Insurance Game' played over the Internet or via 1-800 numbers has shifted the market share. There are too many agents who profess to be advisors but are playing the game for which there is no value. In fact, it has blackened the eye of our profession and made our job more difficult. Now is the time to raise the standards of our profession," he expands.

"I get it. The best price insurance game is a dead-end street. Instead we must become expert risk managers," Tony says.

"It is better to assist people in their endeavors by transferring risk through guiding principles," Ned says. "These guiding principles will set you apart by making you an expert advisor.

"In addition, being an expert and acting as an insurance advisor at all times will have great impact on your personal life, as well as your business life, by freeing you from the bondage imposed by your profession. So, keep your seat belts buckled. I am going to rock your paradigms," he imparts.

"Ned, I am afraid you are going to make Tony cry," Darko quips.

"Maybe you should become a comedian and forgo your pursuit of a trusted insurance advisor," Tony counters. "Please, move on, Ned."

"Aye, Aye, Tony. This principle tells the client that he or she needs to have an insurance buying strategy that needs to be personalized. I will discuss these two points concurrently," Ned says and then transitions.

"People buy insurance for many years. Most people will buy insurance without interruption for their entire lifetime. What other products are there that you buy without interruption for your entire life?"

"Your heat, phone, electricity. You know, the essentials," Darko responds.

"Good answer, but you forgot food," Ned winks.

"Seriously, though, consider that word: essential. Throughout mankind's history, food, clothing, and shelter have always been the essentials. The industrial era was no different except that more essential costs were added. The industrial era brought the need for schools, roads and other services that taxes provide, thus making taxes another essential.

"The industrial era also saw the emergence of a middle class with the need for personal insurance," Ned continues. "One difference between the essentials you described and insurance is that insurance is an intangible product that is bought without interruption for your entire life. The other difference is that most people will spend more money on insurance than any other product they buy over their lifetime.

"In today's world, if you have a desire and need to go forward financially, you must purchase insurance in order to transfer your inevitable risk, and it better be the right insurance—tailored and suitable for each individual and family," Ned postulates.

"Food, clothing, shelter, taxes and insurance. Interesting view," Darko says.

"More than just interesting, Darko," Ned says. "These are hard cold facts."

"My belief is that insurance is the financial foundation for all of your clients. Consider this: a grossly uninsured or under-insured loss can irrefutably lead a family or individual to financial ruin or, at the very least, have devastating effects.

"This reality, this truth, forces me to consider insurance the absolute financial foundation for all of my clients. It forces me to develop an insurance buying strategy that is tailored to the individual needs of my clients. It is unacceptable for me to look at insurance from any other perspective," Ned explains.

"It is unlike the dominating, tired and worn out approaches you'll find in the marketplace, where playing the 'Best Price Insurance Game' and marketing, without regard to our clients' true concerns, trivialize and weaken our hallowed industry. I refuse to play by those rules. In fact, my purpose is to change the rules of the game," Ned completes.

"So, you must be an expert in developing an insurance buying strategy that focuses on the individual needs of your clients," Tony says, then asks, "How does the worst-case scenario phenomenon factor in?"

"Before we get started on this discussion, may I suggest you pull over. I really could use a break," Ned says.

"I'll take the next exit. You know, Ned, I've always known you could speak up to 80 miles per hour, but I didn't realize your gusts could reach 120," Darko jokes.

The colleagues take a break from their insurance discussion and engage in a lighthearted chitchat as they proceed to the next off ramp. Upon returning, they work their way back to Ned's views of the worst-case scenario phenomenon.

"Thanks, Darko, I needed a break. Those gusts were starting to hurt my lips," Ned chuckles, ready to discuss the worst-case scenario insurance phenomenon.

"The original public need for personal insurance was to insure a home against the peril of fire," Ned begins. "Over time, the needs for personal insurance expanded.

"Automobiles created additional insurance needs. This, coupled with the increased availability of credit, created greater needs requiring more sophisticated solutions. These factors, as well as the uncertainty of life, created even more consumer needs. The worst-case scenario is a phenomenon that drives the market and, therefore, dictates the solution. Despite complicated realities, insurance itself is still simple: it safeguards against financial ruin," he says.

"That is what I try to impress upon my clients," Tony says.

"It isn't enough to try to impress upon your clients the existence of the worst-case scenario, Tony; you have to drive it home in order to fulfill your obligation as their trusted insurance advisor," Ned reminds him. "There is no other way. Be accountable from the outset, so that you don't have to become accountable to your clients and their attorneys after-the-fact. Your obligation is to take care of the claim before the claim happens.

"People want to hear about this worst-case scenario insurance loss phenomenon, not flexible payment options, sophisticated websites, or superior customer service," Ned expands.

"They really want to know what will happen if they are severely injured, suffer or cause a fatality in a car accident, or return from a night out to find their house has burned to the ground. They want to know money will be available during these trying times. It is during these times that they will find out if their agent had done his or her job.

"These stark realities make me believe that it's our job and obligation as their advisor to make them aware of the enormous financial risks that lie in front of them on a minute-by-minute and day-to-day basis," he continues.

"You cannot only impress this upon your clients, you have to hit them over the head with it to convince them of these realities. You must hold yourself accountable. If you don't hold yourself accountable, someday, others will."

"I definitely get your point," Tony says. "I will cease trying to impress and, instead, work towards convincing my clients of these realities."

"Thank you, Tony," Ned responds.

"I concur as well," Darko adds. "I have experienced some worst-case scenarios of my own."

"I'm trying to convince you that the advice and coverage you provide clients will not concern hundreds of dollars or even thousands of dollars, but tens of thousands, hundreds of thousands, and in some cases, millions of dollars," Ned says.

"Therefore, I believe that whenever you are advising people you must assume that the worst-case scenario is inevitable. The worst-case scenario perspective will make your clients shift their concern from required coverage to needed coverage. Selling insurance is telling people that they must put risk and risk transfer in its proper perspective," he convinces.

"I will have to admit that I don't always consider the worst-case scenario phenomenon when I discuss a client's insurance portfolio," Darko contributes.

"Your admission is admirable. You do have a conscience, after all," Ned teases before continuing.

"I will also admit that I haven't always considered the worst-case scenario phenomenon but a couple of experiences have strengthened my convictions and made clear the awesome responsibility I accept when handling someone's insurance. These stories are a directive about the absolute need to always place insurance with the worst-case scenario in mind," he says.

"One of these worst-case scenario losses was an excellent long time insured who suffered a total fire loss. After returning home one Sunday afternoon from a matinee showing at our local theater, she found her house surrounded by fire trucks putting out the final flames. Needless to say, nothing was saved. The good news, though, was that we met six months earlier and had increased her overall coverage by $100,000, while raising her deductible to help compensate for the increased cost. The deductible was never mentioned, never even considered. But the increase in coverage we provided is still lauded years later. This client spread the good word and has been an enormous advocate of our agency ever since."

"I have a total fire loss pending right now and, frankly, I am anxious to see the final reconstruction costs," Darko relates. "The house was less than two years old and built in a tract development. I am finding out that it is more expensive to build a house individually than in a mass production tract style. Based on this experience, your worst-case scenario discussion is really hitting home."

"That can't be any fun," Tony says.

"I hope this one works out," says Darko, "but it certainly weighs on me."

"I think you'll be fine, Darko, because it doesn't appear that this house will be grossly under-insured," Ned comforts. "However, there are no doubt cases like this that will always bring anxiety to you and your operation."

"Our biggest concern is underinsuring people for their liability," Ned states. "Areas of coverage that have the greatest worst-case scenario exposures are uninsured motorist coverage and people with no life insurance.

"Another significant conviction builder was an accident involving one of my relatives. During a major Sierra snowstorm my relative was involved in a horrific accident that left a 32-year old father dead. Fortunately, we had written $250,000 per person with a $500,000 occurrence limit and, even of greater consequence, an additional $1,000,000 umbrella. This was of great benefit to my relatives as they were not forced to sell off property and none of their income was levied due to a judgment in excess of their insurance.

"More importantly, there was $1,500,000 dollars provided to the pregnant widow who was left alone to raise two small children. I realize insurance will not bring the father back, but it will help to raise these children.

"What a sad story," Tony says reflecting on this story and the human face it put on his duties within the insurance business. "It is not just a job, it involves the lives of people. I am responsible, not only for my clients, but to the people affected by my clients' loss, perhaps people I have never even met."

"This past year we had an uninsured motorist claim where a stay-at-home mom was involved in a head-on collision with another driver. Our client, who happens to be a personal friend, was severely injured, endured at least two major surgeries, and was left with permanent injures.

"The other party had fallen asleep at the wheel and crossed the line into our insured's path. The negligent party had limits of only 100/300. This case is still pending, but I can rest assured knowing that we provided my client, and friend, with an uninsured motorist limit of $500, 000," Ned finishes.

"Those are definitely eye-opening stories," Tony reaffirms. "I promise to begin selling insurance from this worst-case scenario perspective from this day forward. Any other approach would be illogical and irrational."

"You're right, it is illogical and irrational to look at insurance from any other perspective," Ned says. "I don't ask people about their insurance, I tell and advise them about their insurance. I am here to design a program that takes into consideration that their insurance is their absolute financial foundation. I provide them with expertise that will enable them to transfer their overwhelming risk by implementing a sound insurance buying strategy designed to safeguard them against financial ruin.

"This is what people want to hear and talk about. They want me to eliminate their choices and tell them what they need. After all, that is the service my clients pay for," Ned says and then remembers a Latin phrase, "*Caveat emptor.*"

"Bless you," jokes Darko.

Ned laughs and then translates, "It means 'let the buyer beware.' As trusted insurance advisors, we have a great responsibility to avoid *caveat emptor* at all times. *Caveat emptor* is to shirk your responsibility. Don't provide your clients with options and choices; this will only confuse them. Instead, provide solutions. They are not the expert; you are. This is irrefutable," Ned finishes.

Ned, moving through his presentation with ease, can see that Tony and Darko are already learning some significant lessons they can apply. The worst-case scenario insurance loss phenomenon has left an indelible impression on both of the students.

Chapter 3 Summary

- In this chapter we discuss the second principle of the declaration of intent: *We help [our clients] develop an insurance buying strategy that is tailored to their individual needs and provide them with the protection they need in the event of a worst case scenario.*
- Before you are an expert advisor you must be able to:
  - Design and implement an insurance buying strategy for your clients
  - Tailor the buying strategy to the individual needs of the client
  - Accept the premise that the primary purpose of an insurance program is to safeguard against a worst-case scenario insurance loss
- If you are not an expert advisor, the only game available to you is the 'Best Price Insurance Game.' Playing the 'Best Price Insurance Game' makes you a retailer, not an advisor.
- Insurance is the one thing most people will buy without interruption for their entire lives.
- A grossly uninsured or under-insured loss can irrefutably lead a family or individual to financial ruin or, at the very least, have devastating effects. This makes insurance the absolute financial foundation for all of your clients.
- Whenever you are advising, you must assume that the worst-case scenario is inevitable. The worst-case scenario perspective will make your clients shift their concern from required coverage to needed coverage.
- The biggest concern is underinsuring people for their liability. Areas of coverage that have the greatest worst-case scenario exposures are uninsured motorist coverage and people with no life insurance.
- As a trusted insurance advisor you are responsible, not only for your clients, but to the people affected by your clients' loss, perhaps people you have never even met.

CHAPTER 4

THE FOUR PERILS OF INSURANCE

Neither Tony nor Darko have considered themselves experts in any field before now. They are starting to realize that they no longer need to provide their clients with an array of choices, but instead, only one solution to their insurance needs. Insurance is too great a financial risk to consider anything less than the worst-case scenario.

As they are pondering over these thoughts, Ned asks, "Have either of you ever considered why people need to buy insurance in the first place?"

Tony and Darko, still struck by the enormity their advisement has on their clients' livelihood and future, turn to Ned. They refrain from answering the question and, instead, Darko asks Ned his opinion.

"Why do *you* think people need to buy insurance?" Darko asks.

Ned replies, "It came to me about ten years ago. I was cross-selling clients, as well as trying to obtain new clients, in order to increase my revenues and referrals. It was kind of working, but I wasn't happy or fulfilled. I was going in too many directions.

"I found cross-selling and marketing to be a very difficult and reactive process. Instead of reacting, I wanted to *respond* to the marketplace. At this time, I formulated an all-lines comprehensive presentation, in which I would discuss all the policies a person had in their portfolio. The problem with this approach was that it was not seamless.

"I realized that if I could start discussing insurance as a single product, then I would be more effective. So, I went through and found that when you break down all insurance coverage and policies, there are four perils that people face. Then it came to me: people need to buy insurance to protect against these four perils."

"I hate to interrupt," Darko interjects, "but what are the four perils? Fire, lightning, and these types of things?"

"Those are definitely perils, since peril is defined as 'an imminent danger and the exposure to the risk of harm or loss.' But, the perils you mentioned are specific perils. The perils I am referring to are more general and all-encompassing," Ned responds.

"So, what did you come up with?" Tony asks.

"I didn't come up with anything," Ned retorts. "This is serious business, we're not selling vacuum cleaners; therefore, you should never 'come up' with anything. You must always approach insurance logically and never underestimate the products you sell. 'Coming up' with something has a haphazard implication."

Tony, feeling chastised, sheepishly says, "I'm sorry."

"Don't be sorry, Tony," Ned says. "I wasn't attempting to scold you. I was only emphasizing the seriousness of these matters. It is my belief that the more serious you take this, the better chance you will have for success. Having awareness of these four perils—**property insurance, lawsuit exposure, medical insurance and loss of income**—benefits, not only you, but especially the client.

"With absolute certainty, entering into a discussion of the four perils is a sensible way of breaking down the consequences individuals and families face today, and leads us to our third principle,

> *We bring to our client's attention the financial exposures they have regarding the four insurance perils: property insurance, lawsuit exposure, medical insurance and loss of income."*

Darko naively interjects, "The loss of income peril wouldn't be the most critical peril if it's your house that burns down."

"That's true, Darko," Ned responds, "All the perils are very critical. If your house burns down the most critical peril to you would be property peril, but what if as your house burns down and you simultaneously lose your life? What then would be the most important peril to your family?"

"I get it," Darko says. "You're right again."

"We can't predict or see into the future," Ned continues. "Not knowing what will happen is precisely why we need to buy insurance. I've been around this business long enough to know that it is not a matter of *if* it will happen, but *when*.

"This stark reality causes me to sell insurance with the assumption that the *when* is inevitable. Furthermore, I have taken the hardline stance that looking at this any other way is gross negligence."

"Strong words—gross negligence," Darko says. "You use that expression often."

"They are strong words, Darko, but since insurance is one's financial foundation, again, I believe I must always approach it from the perspective of the worst case scenario; therefore, any other approach I consider to be gross negligence," Ned says.

"In addition, we all face perils in our day to day lives and one of the greatest perils we all face is financial ruin due to improper insurance coverage. As we're discussing each peril I want you to consider each peril from the worst-case scenario perspective, too.

"The first peril is the **property peril.** This is the peril that most people relate to regarding their insurance. In my opinion, this is the most basic and simplistic of all the four perils," Ned continues.

"Property peril coverage is found in all of our clients' insurance portfolios. For example, the auto policy addresses property peril through comprehensive and collision coverage and the uninsured motorist property damage. Rental car coverage also falls under property peril. A boat owner's policy and a recreational vehicle policy contain the property peril in their comprehensive and collision coverage. The homeowner's policy deals most significantly with the property peril and is the most consequential dwelling coverage. For nearly everyone, having their house or apartment burn to the ground would be the worst case scenario regarding the property peril."

"I get it," Tony says. "When discussing the property peril this way, you are able to discuss all of the client's coverage and policies."

"Exactly, Tony," says Ned, "Insurance is one product, with four primary components and these components are the four perils. This is irrefutable.

"In my opinion the entire industry, from agents to companies to claims adjustors, places excessive emphasis on this peril class," Ned says. "Although all peril classes are important and significant, the property peril is easy for people to understand. The values are easy to determine.

"I determine these values with the customer and then move on to the other three perils. Another way of looking at the property peril is that banks and lenders require this coverage; therefore, people need to purchase them. Property coverage is more tangible than the other three perils. People can see their house and drive their cars. They want their boat replaced if it sinks."

Ned continues, "While property peril coverage is required, I am more concerned with the coverage that is most needed and of greatest consequence to my clients. This coverage is found in the other three perils."

"So, you are telling us that, for the most part, property peril coverage is required, but is not the most needed," Darko chimes in. "This makes no sense to me."

"Well, that's because you're stubborn, Darko," Ned says playfully. "What I mean is that required coverage protects the banks and financial institutions. On the other hand, the other three perils protect people and families."

"Medical insurance, lawsuit exposure, and loss of income - these are the real, significant perils people face, and I believe it is my job as their insurance advisor to explain in detail the potential consequences of overlooking these perils. Ascending to the advisor position can only be achieved by discussing the complete needs of your customer. Anything less, I consider being negligent. Does this make sense to you, Darko?"

"It's starting to come to me; I think I am just vested in the way I'm used to selling insurance," Darko says.

"You are, Darko, and I am trying to help you make changes. Willingness to make change as well as managing oneself is essential to success," Ned says. Darko nods, remembering their conversation at the beginning of the trip.

"The existence of the four perils and the irrefutable exposure my clients have to them is the core to fulfilling my mission or purpose in my clients' lives. Again, I am not acting as an advisor, nor am I living up to my obligation as their advisor if I do not discuss these four perils," Ned concludes.

Tony jumps in to say, "I assume you are now going to discuss the **medical insurance peril**."

"That's right," Ned says.

"Many people have medical insurance through their jobs and, if they do, is there any need to discuss this peril?" Tony inquires.

"Excellent point and question," Ned says. "The answer is, yes. As I just said, I don't believe I am acting as their advisor unless I discuss all four perils."

"My mind is open—enlighten me with your rhetoric," Darko quips.

"Medical insurance is certainly a financial risk, since, without medical insurance, an individual could be faced with a costly illness and risk losing significant assets," Ned says. "However, in my opinion, the greatest risk regarding medical insurance is the life and death consequence of having the wrong medical insurance."

"What do you mean? What is having the wrong medical insurance?" Darko asks. "Don't all plans have unlimited lifetime benefits?"

"Yes, under the Affordable Care Act (ACA) they now have unlimited lifetime benefits," Ned interjects, "but, the risk lies in choosing the wrong plan with the wrong network."

Tony chimes in, "Well, isn't that something we can help with, as advisors?"

"Exactly, Tony!" Ned applauds him. "Insurance advisors who sell health insurance will need to be authorities on the nuances and complexities of the ACA, because your clients need help navigating through this new and uncharted system."

"The rollout of the ACA was rife with problems and unforeseen complications," he goes on. "A major problem was that the consumer was encouraged to go online and pick a plan, but nearly all consumers had no idea what they were doing in terms of subsidies and tax implications.

"Health insurance is far too complicated for the layman to conquer," he continues. "We must learn the ins and outs of the new system and use this knowledge to appropriately advise our clients on which network and plan to choose.

"Furthermore, I believe all my clients should have a preferred provider organization, or PPO, with a strong national provider network. I am vehemently opposed to health maintenance organizations, or HMO's, since they constrict a patient's ability to choose the doctors and hospitals they may need in order to save the lives of their family members or themselves," Ned offers.

"What did you mean by that statement?" Tony questions.

"I meant that with an HMO you first have to go to your primary care physician for all illnesses and conditions," Ned responds. "Then, after consulting with them, you may be referred to a specialist.

"With a PPO you can go directly to a specialist. The point is that HMO's are far more bureaucratic than PPO's. I don't want my clients caught up in bureaucracy any more than they have to be, especially when they are dealing with their health and well-being."

"Interesting. I've looked at HMO's as good for a client since they have low out-of-pocket cost," Tony adds.

"That's a fallacy," Ned says. "There is a low out of pocket cost for covered services, however, the premiums are significantly higher than traditional plans, and my philosophy is that my clients should save on their monthly premiums and assume more low-end risk through a health savings account, commonly referred to as an HSA. Remember, the best way to buy insurance is to assume the maximum low-end risk so that you can transfer the insurmountable risk.

"Tony, I brought an example of an HSA and HMO comparison, so you could see for yourself."

"Wow, that's impressive; I never looked at it from 'the out of pocket' perspective," Tony says.

"No offense, Tony, but is there any other way to look at this scenario?" Ned says. "There is no case you'll find where an HMO is superior to an HSA. None. This is irrefutable."

"Irrefutable. There goes that word again," Darko observes.

"That's right, Darko. Irrefutable is a powerful word that builds binding trust with your clients," Ned says.

"Using this word gives you instant accountability. I believe too many agents take the short sighted *caveat emptor* approach. I am not afraid to make myself accountable. In fact, I demand this of myself. The only requirement is that when you use this word your position has to be irrefutable."

Shuffling through his notes in the back seat, Tony questions his new found mentor.

"I am still unclear as to how you discuss the medical peril when your client has a comprehensive benefit package from their work."

"I am glad you brought that up again, Tony," Ned responds.

"Okay, if your client has a benefit package from work, he or she may have an option to choose between an HMO, a traditional plan, or these new HSA's."

"I see. Then you should explain to them the difference between the options and exploit the dangers associated with the HMO's," Tony chimes in.

"Exactly," Ned says.

"Why bother when there is nothing in it for you?" Darko wonders.

"Darko, Darko, Darko. You are disappointing me now," Ned says. "I was starting to think you were coming around and now you go and say something reckless."

"Well, there is only so much time in the day," Darko rebuttals. "How do you justify the time it will take to explain this to them?"

"I believe we already had this discussion, but repetition is the mother of learning," Ned says. "Remember our mission and purpose, our promise to our clients? Remember the first point of the declaration of intent?"

Gaining confidence, Tony recites, ***"At our agency we handle most or all of your insurance and act as your insurance advisor."***

"Bravo, Tony," Ned says. "Remember, my promise, Darko. You can't quantify the value you create when you advise without regard to your compensation."

"Okay, okay, I get it," Darko says with a concentrated look on his face. "Sometimes, it takes a couple of explanations for it to sink in."

"Darko, your objections help add value to our exercise," Ned reassures. "Taking into account why something should be done when there is nothing in it for you is a valid consideration.

"First, let me state, when you are imparting knowledge or providing expertise there is always something in it for you. Remember, when you give, you always receive in greater quantities," Ned imparts further.

"Your promise, your mission, your noble obligation to your customers should never be compromised. Anytime you stray from this principle you compromise your integrity, and this is fatal.

"One of my agents was conducting a personal insurance review with a lady who was the bookkeeper of a small firm of ten people," Ned expands. "She was in charge of the health insurance for the firm. The end result was the writing of a very nice small group account. The agent was rewarded for his effort, but of greater benefit, the employees were rescued from the perils associated with an HMO.

"In the end, embracing health insurance and fully understanding the Affordable Care Act and its relationship to HMO's, PPO's and HSA's will enhance your reputation and will create great loyalty from your client to yourself," Ned says. "One product, one advisor, one solution."

Darko exalts, "Wow that information alone has been worth the ride. I still like there being something in it for me."

"On that note, Darko, let's pull over and stretch our legs, maybe get a soda, and when we get back in the car we'll get started on the next peril, **lawsuit exposure**."

Pulling over Darko says, "Can't wait."

Chapter 4 Summary

- In this chapter, we begin to discuss the third principle of the declaration of intent: ***We bring to our client's attention the financial exposures they have regarding the four insurance perils— property insurance, lawsuit exposure, medical insurance and loss of income.***
- The first peril that people need protect themselves from is the **property peril.**
  - This is the peril that most people relate to regarding their insurance; banks and lenders require property peril coverage.
  - Auto insurance contains the property peril under comprehensive, collision, rental car coverage, and uninsured motorist property damage.
  - A boat owner's policy and a recreational vehicle policy contain the property peril in their comprehensive and collision coverage.
  - The homeowner's policy deals most significantly with the property peril and is the most consequential dwelling coverage. Thus, with the property peril, you are able to discuss all of the client's coverage and policies.
- As an agent, you should be more concerned with the coverage that is of greatest consequence to your clients; this is found under the remaining three perils (medical insurance, lawsuit exposure, and loss of income).
- The second peril is the **medical insurance peril.**
  - The greatest risk regarding medical insurance is the life and death consequence of having the wrong medical insurance.
  - The Affordable Care Act makes it easy for clients to buy health insurance online, but most of the time the system can be too confusing for the layman to understand. They

need an insurance advisor to help them buy the right insurance.

○ Clients should save on their monthly premiums and self-insure through a health savings account commonly referred to as an HSA.

"Living at risk is jumping off the cliff and building your wings on the way down."

- Ray Bradbury

Chapter 5

THE FOUR PERILS OF INSURANCE (continued)

Thankful for the stop, Darko now behind the wheel, the three resume their road trip. Ned seizes the opportunity to impress an objective lesson using their current road trip, "Darko, did you happen to consider that every time you get behind the wheel of this automobile, any automobile, that you are putting your entire financial future at risk?"

"Not exactly, but if I drove like you, I probably would think a little more about it," Darko kids.

"Well, if you haven't bought the right insurance for yourself and your family, then you are putting your entire financial future at risk each and every day," Ned says, causing Darko to flinch at the personal application of the conversation.

Ned develops this line of reasoning to encompass all clients, "This reality is the reason we are able to write most of our new accounts. My office believes that most people are grossly under-insured in the area of liability. We believe this because we see it on a daily basis. We see it on their auto declarations, homeowner's policies, and lack of knowledge about an umbrella policy."

"I admit I have seen quite a few examples of people being under-insured when it comes to their liability," Tony contributes.

"This brings us to the third peril, **lawsuit exposure**," Ned says.

"We all know we live in a litigious society. Individuals or families face lawsuit exposure when involved in an accident where bodily injury or property damage occurs. Coverage for lawsuit exposure is found under bodily injury and property damage sections of the auto policy, it is a part of the comprehensive personal liability section of a homeowner's policy, and most significantly, it is found in an umbrella policy. This is something that anybody with an insurance license should recognize," Ned pauses and then continues.

"So, why is it that over time I have found that most—not some—but most individuals and families are grossly under-insured in this area? This is an obvious area of significant coverage but being under-insured is so prevalent that I find it staggering. I really believe there should be industry standards to prevent this crisis."

"A lot of people you talk to just don't believe in it," Tony offers. "You explain it to them and they still don't get it."

"I don't buy this for one minute," Ned says. "There are some people who don't believe in insurance, but they aren't homeowners. When you explain to people they could lose equity in their home or that their future wages can be levied due to being under-insured, I promise you, logically and emotionally they will be involved in your discussion. You would be surprised how involved people get in comprehensive insurance discussions when you speak directly and candidly with them.

"It is an advisor's duty and responsibility to explain to clients the risks involved in being uninsured or under-insured," Ned adds. "You must set the tone for your entire presentation. Agents are always telling me that the liability exposures of their clients are important to them and are discussed. If they are telling me the truth, then why is it that most people have major gaps in this area of coverage?

"In today's marketplace, you'll find homeowners who have $100,000 per person limits with a $300,000 occurrence limit on their auto policy. These are, most times, paltry limits of insurance," Ned finishes.

"Wow, you really get fired up when you discuss liability insurance. You really are passionate about this subject," Tony says.

"You are darn right!" Ned exhorts. "I am passionate about all insurance. Remember: one product, one advisor, one solution. I actually see red and my veins pop. That is why I demand that my clients place the suitable coverage. I make no exceptions! I know that exceptions only diminish the value of my philosophy as their insurance advisor.

"In fact, I will go so far as to say that it is downright stupid to assume any risk in the area of liability insurance. If an agent can't explain this to his clients and prospects, he or she should look for another vocation. I can tell you this—nearly all of our new clients are written because my agents and I are able to find grossly uninsured exposures in their existing insurance portfolios," Ned completes.

"I know one thing, I don't want to be downright stupid," Darko says.

Ned, sensing that Darko is feeling overwhelmed by the insurgence of new ideas, turns to him to explain.

"I only go over the top with my comments to make significant points. With that said, I do believe it is irrational and illogical and, once again, downright stupid to not carry the absolute appropriate amount of liability insurance.

"With this belief, diagnosing my client's exposure to the financial risk of lawsuit exposure is the initial thrust of my presentation and this is where I am able to demonstrate my overall competence. It substantiates my strong and unwavering conviction about developing a sound strategy designed to protect their future income and assets," Ned adds.

He then confidently declares, "By the end of our journey, my hope is that both of you will have built convictions to choose a path that will help you fulfill your goal of becoming a trusted insurance advisor. You will find that once you have achieved this, the only thing left will be for you to exercise the discipline that it takes to do the absolute right thing, all of the time, for all of your clients.

"Doing the absolute right thing for all of your clients, all of the time, includes discussing the final peril, **loss of income**, and is what I believe to be the most essential peril for us to consider," Ned says.

"This is the area of coverage that protects an individual or family from a loss of income due to either death or disability. This coverage is provided through life and disability policies, and also it is in the uninsured and under-insured motorist coverage of auto policies."

"I never considered the uninsured motorist to have a link to life and disability coverage, but I certainly will in the future," Darko says.

"You will, Darko, because I've taught you that insurance is one product made up of various components," Ned reminds him.

"By accepting the reality of single product insurance, an advisor provides one single solution divided into four perils."

"Hmm. One Product, one advisor, one solution. There goes that adage again," Tony ponders.

"Loss of income, in many cases, is the greatest risk most individuals and families face today. However, I find it the most overlooked and under-insured of all of the four perils. How can this be?" Ned inquires.

"A lot of people just don't seem to get it…but, wait," Tony pauses, considering the short-sighted training he has received during his time as an insurance agent, "the real answer is a lot of people aren't able to get it because agents and companies are not able to explain it in the right context."

"I can see my philosophy is starting to sink in a little," Ned remarks. "The loss of income peril is the greatest exposure most individuals and families face and it all begins with the uninsured motorist.

"With this discussion I begin to win the complete trust and respect of my clients for discussing needed, rather than required, coverage. This is where I bring to the table the so-called 'delicate' discussion of life insurance, which is also a loss of income peril and is of great consequence. It must always be discussed," Ned finishes.

With a pause in the conversation, Tony and Darko consider how the loss of a loved one truly alters the lives of those left behind. Both seem deep in thought and unready to participate in a mutual conversation, so Ned diverges from the topic of death to discuss the history of uninsured motorist coverage.

Ned discusses the contribution of Charles J. Givens during the late 1980's. His views helped him emerge as a leader in personal financial advice. A disciple of his explained Givens' advice about reducing or eliminating uninsured motorist coverage. His stance was that it was a costly and unneeded coverage that could be eliminated in order to save clients' money. Ned turns to Darko and Tony who have mentally returned to the conversation. "That encounter got me logically and emotionally involved. How would you guys define advice that encourages underinsuring in order to save money?

"Using your words, it sounds like reckless and negligent advice, just like the story you told us when we were discussing the worst-case scenario phenomenon," interjects Tony.

"Exactly, it is this advice and the resulting lawsuit that built my conviction and emboldened me, as I knew this was illogical and very bad advice," Ned pauses. "A 1993 lawsuit against Givens from a woman whose husband was killed in a head on collision caused by an uninsured driver exposed his advice to be fraudulent. The woman and her husband had taken Givens' advice and eliminated uninsured motorist protection from their insurance program. Givens' strategy to drop this insurance in order to save money was his ultimate demise, it damaged his credibility to the point that even his obituary contained details of this case," Ned adds.

"What a sad and pathetic legacy to leave," Darko says.

"Yes, that is certain," Ned says.

"Do you feel you need to be provided with any more evidence in order to comprehend the significance of adequate uninsured motorist coverage or does this suffice?" he asks.

"This will suffice," Darko says, slightly consumed by the irrefutability of this evidence.

Ned, seeing that Darko and Tony are feeling the weight of all their conversations, takes the opportunity to encourage and empower them.

"Remember, you are the only person on earth who can use your ability. You are both smart guys and know what it takes to succeed in this business, but it doesn't just happen. You must plan to succeed, educate and prepare yourself for success. Only then can you expect it to come.

"Over time I have learned that men and women are anxious to improve their circumstances and conditions in life but are unwilling to improve themselves," he states.

"In fact, a lot of people just don't take the time to prepare themselves to become a trusted insurance advisor. They are engaged in the constant pursuit of shortcuts. They make excuses as to why they don't read the books they need to read and are forced to make excuses as to why they are unable to transcend their self-imposed limitations.

"I believe that a business that makes nothing but money is a poor business. If money is your hope for independence, you will never have it. The only real security a person has in this world is a reserve of knowledge, experience, and ability. Givens didn't subscribe to these beliefs. He tried to find a shortcut and the shortcut led to his prolific demise.

"I get excited when I think about the opportunities you will produce for yourself and your clients as you implement my declaration of intent into all of your operations," Ned finishes.

The colleagues then move on to discuss life insurance and its place in the loss of income peril.

"I like how you said that life insurance is a delicate discussion," Darko says. "But the discussion about life insurance should not be a delicate discussion, it should be mandatory, especially when there are children and dependents to consider."

"Well spoken, Darko," Ned says. "Consider this: the financial risk families assume when they either have no life insurance, or limited life insurance, is the single greatest assumption of risk most families face. Why do people need life insurance? People need life insurance for the sole and express purpose of replacing income lost when a family member or wage earner dies. It replaces the income and value a family member contributes to a family.

"Discussing life insurance with people is not morbid, pushy, or insensitive, it is essential to providing the financial protection that our declaration of intent promises."

Ned continues, "By demonstrating the enormous financial risk a family has in the area of loss of income, whether it is the uninsured motorist exposure or the life insurance exposure, you will gain the complete trust and respect of your clients. They will come to accept you as their advisor."

"Tell us how you sell them life insurance, for crying out loud," Darko says.

"This will come, Darko," Ned replies. "Remember, you don't put the cart in front of the horse. We haven't completed our discussion of the four perils, nor have we discussed consequential and inconsequential insurance. These discussions will take the entire remainder of our drive to the conference.

On our return trip, we will discuss how to present all of this information in a comprehensive insurance presentation based on the principles and tenets of our declaration of intent," Ned finishes.

"Okay, I guess I'll have to wait," Darko says.

"Be patient," Ned advises. "You've waited your entire life for this information, so what's a couple of more days?"

He then proceeds with his discussion.

"The existence of the four perils makes the auto policy the perfect place to start your comprehensive insurance review, because a unique characteristic of the auto insurance policy is that it alone contains all of the four perils. Bodily injury introduces the *lawsuit exposure*. Uninsured motorist leads to the discussion about *loss of income*. Medical payments bring the *medical insurance* peril to the discussion and, finally, the comprehensive and collision addresses *property peril*.

"This is significant because I am selling concepts to people and my livelihood depends on my ability to explain these concepts in a clear and concise manner. When explaining the four perils I am able to immediately talk about the stuff of consequence. By establishing the four perils in the auto policy, I make the presentation seamless and avoid uncomfortable transitions moving from product to product," Ned says.

"Seamless transitions? I like the sound of that," Tony says before adding, "It sounds a lot better than cross-selling."

"You don't have to cross-sell when you discuss insurance as a single product designed to transfer the risk your clients face today. As a trusted advisor, one who regards insurance as their client's financial foundation, you will follow the edicts of your declaration of intent past the confines of cross-selling," Ned says ready to discuss the first coverage.

"The first coverage you discuss on an auto policy is the bodily injury coverage, which, like home liability or dwelling policy, falls under the lawsuit exposure peril. Therefore, they are one singular financial risk.

"The next coverage you discuss on the auto policy is the uninsured motorist coverage, which falls under the loss of income peril. Life insurance also falls under the loss of income peril; therefore, they are one singular financial risk.

"Down the line you discuss medical payments on the auto policy. This discussion leads you to the discussion of their health insurance, as this coverage falls under the medical insurance peril.

"Finally, the physical damage coverage brings you to the discussion about property peril. You must consider all property peril risks as one singular financial risk. Whether it is the dwelling coverage on their home, physical damage on their automobile, boat, or recreational vehicle, it remains one. This all requires one advisor, one solution, one insurance buying strategy," Ned finishes.

"I like the single-product theory more and more," Tony says. "It is making more sense as our discussion progresses."

"So, you are seeing that by embracing the four perils families and individuals face on a minute-by-minute and day-to-day basis, you will be able to sell concepts and strategies and, at the same time, avoid the arduous and mundane discussion of policies and conditions," Ned says.

"The four perils will assist you in turning your discussion into a seamless and coherent presentation. The perils will help your clients understand insurance as one single product designed to transfer all of their risk," he finishes.

"The four perils are simple for me to understand; therefore, I should be able to explain this to my clients and prospects," adds Darko.

After this discussion, Tony and Darko sit in silent satisfaction knowing and understanding why people need to buy insurance. They are eager to learn more about explaining all these concepts to their clients. They smile at Ned and await his explanation about how clients should buy their insurance and consider the consequences of their insurance purchases.

Chapter 5 Summary

- In this chapter, we continue to discuss the third principle of the declaration of intent: *We bring to our client's attention the financial exposures they have regarding the four insurance perils— property insurance, lawsuit exposure, medical insurance and loss of income.*
- The third peril is **lawsuit exposure**.
  - Individuals or families face lawsuit exposure when involved in an accident where bodily injury or property damage occurs.
  - Coverage for lawsuit exposure is found under bodily injury and property damage sections of the auto policy, it is a part of the comprehensive personal liability section of a homeowner's policy, and most significantly, it is found in an umbrella policy.
  - Most individuals and families are grossly under-insured in this area!
  - Diagnosing your new and existing clients' exposure to the financial risk of lawsuit exposure is how you will be able to demonstrate your overall competence and enable you to develop a sound strategy designed to protect their future income and assets.
- The final peril, **loss of income,** is the most essential peril for us to consider.
  - This is the area of coverage that protects an individual or family from a loss of income due to either death or disability.
  - This coverage is provided through life and disability policies, and also it is in the uninsured and under-insured motorist coverage of auto policies. This is also where you bring up the discussion of life insurance.
  - The financial risk families assume when they either have no life insurance, or limited life insurance, is the single greatest

assumption of risk they face. Life insurance replaces the income and value a family member contributes to a family.

- ◦ By demonstrating the enormous financial risk a family has in the area of loss of income, whether it is the uninsured motorist exposure or the life insurance exposure, you will gain the complete trust and respect of your clients. They will come to accept you as their advisor.
- The auto policy is the perfect place to start your comprehensive insurance review, because it alone contains all of the four perils.
  - ◦ Bodily injury introduces the *lawsuit exposure.*
  - ◦ Uninsured motorist leads to the discussion about *loss of income.*
  - ◦ Medical payments bring the *medical insurance* peril to the discussion.
  - ◦ The comprehensive and collision addresses *property peril.*
- By establishing the four perils in the auto policy, you make the presentation seamless and avoid uncomfortable transitions moving from product to product.

Chapter 6

CONSEQUENTIAL VS. INCONSEQUENTIAL COVERAGE

After a long pause in conversation, Darko exclaims, "Tell me more, tell me more! Enlighten me further. I submit myself to your wisdoms. I am on board with absolutely no resistance."

He surprises his car companions and they all laugh at the change that has occurred in Darko during these discussions.

"Darko, thanks for your enthusiasm," Ned says. "I am glad you are on board."

"No problem here. Please proceed, enlightened one."

Ned smiles and begins a new discussion.

"There are two words we will focus on now: **consequential** and **inconsequential**. I use them to explain the legitimate concerns my clients should consider," Ned says.

He then asks Tony to read the fourth principle of the declaration of intent.

Tony reads as directed,

We find that most people are over-insured where coverage is least needed and under-insured where coverage is most needed.

Darko, a little confused asks, "What do the terms consequential and inconsequential have to do with this statement?"

"Well, when I say most people are over-insured where coverage is least needed, I find that their insurance portfolios are concerned with inconsequential financial occurrences," Ned begins. "When I say most people are under-insured where coverage is most needed, it is because they are grossly under-insured in the areas of greatest financial consequence."

"Understood," Darko says.

"These two words, when applied to insurance, allow me to explain insurance to people in a straightforward and easy to understand manner," Ned continues. "Using these words and explaining them in the right context helps people easily understand what they face and why certain coverage is of greater consequence than others. Therefore, there are areas of coverage that come with consequence and those with inconsequence."

"Well, then, what are these areas?" asks Tony.

"First, understand that these words will give you the opportunity to explain insurance in a practical, logical, and ethical manner," Ned says.

"I have become aware that when I use these two words, they assist me in getting my clients logically and emotionally involved in our discussion. In addition, it assists me in explaining to my clients why they have to buy insurance using a sound financial strategy."

"I thought the four perils were the reason people need to buy insurance," Tony says.

"The four perils explain *what* people need to insure against and the consequential view demonstrates *how* they safeguard themselves against financial ruin," Ned answers.

"After I make people aware of the four financial perils they face, I then break down all insurance coverage into two categories: consequential and inconsequential insurance. In short, the consequential view provides you with a strategy and gives you a directive to buy only consequential coverage."

"So, you first explain the four perils and then start to discuss the areas that are of the greatest consequence?" Tony asks.

"Not quite," Ned says. "Consequential coverage is the coverage that is in place to safeguard against catastrophic events. Inconsequential coverage is coverage for instances in which complete or total loss would not cause financial ruin."

"So, you tell people that, in most cases, you'll find them to be under-insured where coverage is most needed and over-insured where coverage is least needed. Therefore, where coverage is most needed is the consequential coverage and where coverage is least needed is the inconsequential coverage?" Tony clarifies.

"You can refer to consequential coverage in an assortment of words and expressions," Ned says. "I have heard people call consequential coverage 'vital coverage', 'important coverage', or 'significant coverage.' I use over-insured and under-insured, as well as consequential and inconsequential. I believe the words consequential and inconsequential make the greatest impact. To me, words and language are essential to your success," Ned responds.

"Makes perfect sense," Tony says.

Ned nods in encouragement and then moves on.

"Bodily injury is an obvious coverage of great consequence, as the risk of being under-insured in this area could lead to financial ruin. When I am discussing this coverage with people, I explain that this is the area of coverage that protects their assets and future income from a lawsuit. That's why having the absolute, necessary, and appropriate limits in this important category of insurance is mandatory. I am unwavering on this point and believe that there is no logical reason for self-insuring in this area."

"This would fall under the lawsuit exposure peril," Tony offers.

"It appears that you will do well on your midterm," Ned praises. "You are proving to be a competent and engaged listener."

He then continues, "Now, in my estimation, uninsured motorist coverage is yet another obvious coverage of consequence, as being under-insured in this area can also lead to financial ruin. I tell people that underinsuring in this area is irrational and could lead to many real problems. I tell my clients that this is where their future income is safeguarded and that there is enormous financial risk existing in this

50

area. I emphasize the significant financial risk they face every time they get behind the wheel of an automobile or walk the street as a pedestrian. Remember, this coverage follows you as a driver, a passenger or as a pedestrian."

"This would fall under the loss of income peril," Tony chimes in again.

"You insist on scoring points, Tony," Darko says before adding, "I know what perils they fall under as well."

"I am certain that you do, Darko," Ned reassures. "With you, I am not concerned with your understanding of the subject matter, I am most concerned with you adapting to this new way of thinking. After all, you are vested in your old ways. The problem is, old ways of doing things give you the impression that they are working. When, in fact, these old ways shackle and imprison you."

"You are afraid that I will go back to the office and remain a thing, a mere cog in the wheel, but I will prove you wrong," Darko counters.

"Good," Ned says. "I hope you are right. After all is said, the choice is yours."

"Medical payments on an auto policy are not a coverage of consequence as long as the client has medical insurance," he continues. "Since medical payments are a duplication of one's health insurance, I don't recommend them. They will, at best, pay for a person's health insurance deductible. The key here is that assuming some risk in this area will free up the dollars to purchase the proper limits of bodily injury or uninsured motorist, even umbrella coverage if required."

"So, you don't consider medical payments to be a consequential coverage?" Tony asks. "When you discussed medical insurance during the four peril discussion, it seemed to be consequential at that time."

"When we discussed the medical insurance peril, I was discussing health insurance, which is consequential coverage," Ned begins. "We are now discussing medical payment on an auto policy and the maximum coverage limit I have seen on an auto policy is $100,000. Many carriers offer only $5,000 as a maximum limit. Most health insurance policies will have as much as $5 million or more in coverage.

"Taking into account these figures, I believe medical payments on an automobile insurance policy are inconsequential; but health insurance is consequential," he explains.

"Medical payments on an auto policy also create servicing problems in the agency," Darko adds. "You always have doctors and chiropractors calling your office for payments and other issues."

"This is true, Darko," Ned replies. "I would rather not place the coverage because the benefits are limited and the protection is inconsequential. I believe it is better to advise the client to save premiums in this area of coverage so they can afford to spend the premiums in areas of greater consequence.

"An auto policy's limited medical payments render this coverage inconsequential."

"Since we are discussing the auto policy, my guess is that physical damage coverage would also be inconsequential coverage. Am I right?" Tony asks.

"You are right again, Tony," Ned praises. "Comprehensive and collision, in my opinion, is inconsequential. Collision is a required coverage if there is a lien on the car; therefore, it is a significant coverage.

"However, based on my definition of consequential loss—those areas of coverage in place to safeguard against financial ruin—I believe that physical damage coverage has been misrepresented as the most consequential of all coverage on an auto policy. I would estimate that 95 percent of all physical damage claims are merely inconveniences. For the most part, auto insurance is marketed and sold in order to cover physical damage.

"Companies talk about repair costs, aftermarket parts, and windshield coverage. Agents discuss deductible buybacks, the quality of their companies' physical damage adjusters, windshield coverage, and bold promises about their quick response to claims. This is a shortsighted, illogical, irrational approach. It encourages people to spend extra money and time discussing insurance that lacks consequence.

"Tell me this, would you be more concerned with the quick response to an inconsequential claim or the competent response to a claim of great consequence?" Ned pauses as Tony interjects.

"I would much rather have competent responses to a claim of great consequence," he responds. "I guess you can't have a competent response to a claim of great consequence if you don't have the proper coverage in place at the time of the loss."

"Exactly. For this reason I direct my customers to purchase high deductibles and remove physical damage coverage from most vehicles over seven years old or with high mileage," Ned takes a breath and continues.

"It seems a complete waste of time to discuss inconsequential events at the expense of building an insurance buying strategy for your clients that protects them in the event people are killed or severely injured in auto accidents. I find these situations to be of much greater consequence than a loss of a few thousand dollars on a vehicle, a home, or a medical insurance claim.

"That's the difference between an insurance advisor like myself and an agent or company that happens to have a license to sell insurance policies. Discussing inconsequential coverage in an insurance program should be used as a catalyst to discuss the coverage that truly matters," Ned imparts.

"The following analogy puts this in a more logical, ethical and proper perspective," he continues.

"If you were to suffer a total loss on a later model vehicle without comprehensive and collision coverage and you owed, let's say, $20,000 on the vehicle, this could be a financial hardship but most people could and would survive this scenario financially," he begins.

"However, if someone were involved in an accident where a fatality or severe bodily injury occurred with a collision deductible of $500 and limits of 100/300 on bodily injury coverage, this would financially ruin most people and affect them for a lifetime.

"I am not suggesting self-insuring late model vehicles; however, I am exposing the grave consequence of suffering a grossly under-insured loss. As an insurance advisor, my purpose and intent is to prepare my clients for the worst case scenario," Ned adds.

"I have to admit to spending too much time discussing inconsequential insurance coverage and not enough on the real issues my clients should consider," Tony says. "I can see that using and understanding these two words will help me explain insurance more effectively."

"That is for certain," Darko affirms. "I can't wait to get started."

"Inconsequential coverage will help your client understand that insurance is not for minor losses," Ned recaps. "It will exploit the weakness of their existing coverage and help us provide insurance that is the financial foundation to our clients. Coverage of consequence safeguards them against financial ruin caused by one of the four financial perils."

All men nod in agreement and Ned begins another lecture.

"Consequential and inconsequential permit me to describe coverage and limits in a clear and concise manner. It defines me as an insurance advisor. When I sit down with a person or a couple and review their insurance portfolio, most often I find consequential gaps in their insurance portfolio. I emphasize that the entire agency and I are here to provide them with a logical insurance buying strategy and give them sound, professional advice that will assist them in buying the right insurance to protect all their assets, future income and lifestyle against the four financial perils. I feel we are here to do more than just sell them insurance at the lowest price."

"Amen to that," Darko interrupts.

"The insurance buying strategy first demonstrates the existence of the four perils and then uses the consequential/inconsequential view to determine where the emphasis of coverage should lie," Ned resumes.

"First, I direct the person to select higher deductibles and trim the inconsequential coverage, such as rental car coverage, medical payments, and maybe some floater coverage. Then, I can take these savings to finance the purchasing of coverage that is of real consequence. This includes: bodily injury, uninsured motorist, umbrella, and, of course, life insurance.

"By directing people with the sound advice to assume more risk, I am able to deliver the coverage of consequence, often times, at a similar or lower cost to what they were paying, since most prospects will have low deductibles or a program overburdened with inconsequential coverage and associated costs," Ned says.

"I have needed these answers in the past," Darko says. "The knowledge you are sharing with us has exceeded my expectations. I am starting to understand that even I can make a difference."

"Of course you can make a difference," Ned says fondly. "I have great faith in you, Darko."

Ned continues, "The insurance industry's recent product innovations of offering deeper discounts than ever before and their high deductible options are a signal that this is the direction to take. They are also designing new products that are eliminating some of the inconsequential and costly coverage.

"I started looking at this whole endeavor as a tri-lateral agreement, or partnership between the client, the company, and, most importantly, myself, wherein we all agree to participate in this transfer of risk.

"The client's responsibility is to assume the suitable amount of risk they can afford. This in turn will create greater responsibility on their part to prevent loss, as their participation in a loss is greater than before. However, their reward will be to benefit by having insurance coverage with deeper limits and greater shields.

"The insurance company's responsibility is to allow the customer to transfer their overwhelming risk to them in exchange for a premium. Attracting more prudent, responsible customers will lead the insurance company to the rewards of greater profits.

"I have the final and greatest responsibility in this tri-lateral pact. My responsibility is heavier because I must provide the expertise, through preparation and education, to manage my client's risk. Providing expertise has allowed me to transcend from an agent to a trusted insurance advisor and earn greater profits to achieve increased esteem.

"All of this from two words: consequential and inconsequential. When applied to insurance it has allowed me to explain insurance in a straight forward, easy to understand manner. In conclusion, we are all selling the same products, so what gives one agent an advantage over another?"

Both Darko and Tony ponder this question, considering all the information they have received. They recall this question being posed at the beginning of the trip. They look to Ned to reinforce and build on these ideas.

"To me, it's quite simple," Ned reveals. "It is our ability to demonstrate and prove our level of competence and expertise. This comes down to our verbal communication. Language is everything. I know that success has many components but our ability to communicate is essential to our success. It has been said that the limits of your language are the limits of your world!"

The colleagues pass a mileage sign and realize the drive to the conference is near the end. Tony is happy, considering that this drive has been better than he imagined. The time has flown by and he has learned so much. Darko looks over at Tony's beaming face and considers his initial disdain towards Tony's enthusiasm and realizes that, for the first time in years, he does not have to search for job satisfaction—it has been building on the drive and now is bubbling at the surface.

Ned looks at his confident devotees and sees that they are eager to begin applying the things they are learning. He is proud of the journey they have made thus far, and is excited to continue the lessons. He realizes the true test of making a choice and following through still lies ahead, as he thinks about the final thoughts he wants to instill before they arrive at the conference.

Chapter 6 Summary

- This chapter discusses the fourth principle of the declaration of intent: *We find that most people are over-insured where coverage is least needed and under-insured where coverage is most needed.*

- The four perils explain **what** people need to insure against and the consequential/inconsequential view—where insurance is most and least needed—demonstrates **how** they safeguard themselves against financial ruin.

- The consequential/inconsequential view directs clients to buy only consequential coverage, which is the coverage that is in place to safeguard against catastrophic events.

- Inconsequential coverage is coverage for instances in which complete or total loss would not cause financial ruin. (Examples: *medical payments on an auto policy, comprehensive and collision,* and *rental car coverage.)*

- In most cases, you'll find people to be under-insured where coverage is most needed (consequential) and over-insured where coverage is least needed (inconsequential).

- Areas of great consequence that could lead to financial ruin are: *bodily injury* and *uninsured motorist.*

- The client's responsibility is to assume the suitable amount of risk they can afford. This in turn will create greater responsibility on their part to prevent loss, as their participation in a loss is greater than before.

- The insurance company's responsibility is to allow the customer to transfer their overwhelming risk to them in exchange for a premium.

- The agent has the final and greatest responsibility in this **tri-lateral pact**. Your responsibility is greater because you must provide the expertise, through preparation and education, to manage your client's risk.

"My business is not prognosis, but diagnosis. I am not engaged in therapeutics, but in pathology."

- H. L. Mencken

CHAPTER 7

DIAGNOSIS AND PROGNOSIS

The men, though near the exit to the conference, make one more stop. They are all are visibly relieved. Although the trip has been made light and interesting through the exchange of dialogue, they are eager to get to their destination.

This is especially true of Darko and Tony who are anticipating the conference and the opportunity it will afford them to compare the information they have been receiving with the information they are about to get. They hope to see how they work together. Both men are grateful for their newfound focus and are happy that they are in the right frame of mind for the conference.

"Before our ride, I'll admit, deep down I was a little bit afraid," Tony says. "It's hard to be new in this business. I find that, despite all my hopefulness, my future still seemed too uncertain, but our discussion gives me new confidence. Your teachings have come at the right time, and I believe, in the right place. I'm ready for the rest of the ride."

"I am of the same mind, Tony," Darko agrees.

"You guys know me by now, I am ready to roll," Ned, his eyes twinkling at their enthusiasm, easily revs up for the new discussion, but first a break.

Upon returning to the car, Ned goes directly into the fifth principle,

"We diagnose [our clients'] exposure to the four financial perils and then help them obtain suitable coverage.

The operative word in this statement is 'diagnose,'" he says. "In order for me to fulfill my obligations set forth in my declaration of intent and satisfy my conscience, I must diagnose my clients' exposures to the four irrefutable financial perils. It is much the same as a doctor. Can you imagine a doctor trying to treat an illness that he has not yet diagnosed? Unthinkable—prognosis without diagnosis is malpractice.

"In our own profession, it is very similar," he continues. "Whereas the medical industry protects people's physical health, our purpose is to protect the financial health of our clients. In order to give clients the proper 'prescription,' first we must diagnose their exposure to the four perils. Once I have done this I am in a better position to protect the financial well-being of my clients.

"My standard is simple. Placing insurance without diagnosing the clients' exposure is insurance malpractice. This is yet another step in gaining my clients' respect, trust and logic. They understand the financial risks they face and, in turn, I am able to satisfy my conscience."

"You are still making sense," Darko interjects. "Please expand."

"Once I have gone through my mission statement, I immediately begin a diagnosis of the four financial perils," Ned says.

"So, you actually say your entire declaration of intent, just as I have read it aloud on our ride to the conference?" Tony questions.

"Not quite," Ned replies. "I am so comfortable with and have absolute conviction in my declaration of intent, that when I go over it, I am speaking from the heart. Often times it is a paraphrased, genuine version. You definitely don't want your declaration of intent to sound canned or like a pitch. It is a belief. It is a purpose. It is from the heart."

Ned pauses and then delivers an example of his heartfelt pledge.

"At my agency we handle most or all of our clients' insurance and act as their insurance advisor. We consider insurance to be the financial foundation to our clients. Your income, assets and personal property are at risk to four financial perils. We need to diagnose what your exposures are to these financial risks and then we will be able to assist you in transferring the risk that you face.

"After diagnosing your exposures, I will help you establish a sound insurance buying strategy that is designed to protect you against the perils associated with the worst-case scenario insurance loss. I find that most people I meet with will be under-insured in the areas where coverage is most needed and they will be over-insured in the areas where coverage is least needed," he finishes.

"Where do you go from there?" Tony asks.

Sensing Tony's complete attention and anticipation, Ned, always filled with a sense of humor, deadpans, "I normally get anxious at this point. Many times, I fumble around a little bit. Sometimes, I even break into a cold sweat, but, normally, I am able to recover enough to deliver my comprehensive insurance presentation."

"Really?" Tony is not only incredulous, but slightly panicked.

"I'm kidding! I was trying to make you nervous, Tony."

"Thanks a lot," Tony says. "I'm glad you were joking. I was starting to feel as though there would always be a high level of anxiety."

"Anxiety comes from lack of knowledge," Ned tells him. "Prior to our last discussion, with all due respect, you were not certain of what you were going to say in each presentation. If I were to have asked you what it is that you do, your response would have been vague. It would have been unremarkable and unmemorable."

"I'll have to admit, it would've been," Tony responds.

"But now, when you go back to your office and respond with something like what I just stated, you'll be much more confident in asking a client to sit down and allow you to diagnose their exposures to the four perils. Then, you will be able to implement a long-term insurance buying strategy that views insurance as one single financial product," Ned says.

Tony confidently practices the declaration of intent.

"Excellent, Tony," Ned says. "Now, you give it a try, Darko."

Darko takes a turn at it and then wonders, "All right, where do you go from there?"

"In order to proceed, you need some personal finance information and combined family income," Ned starts.

"Without hesitation, after completing the declaration of intent, you immediately discuss their personal finances?" Darko asks.

"Yes, Darko," Ned says. "I complete my declaration of intent and then I begin to ask them about all their personal finances. I need this information before I can move on. Remember, prognosis without diagnosis is malpractice. I tell my clients that their assets and future income are at risk to the four financial perils, and this is the sole reason that they will need to buy insurance.

"You will find that, after you deliver a clear and concise positioning statement to your clients, your clients will be more than willing to share this information with you. Most people understand that their personal financial information is vital to this discussion."

"I agree with all that you have said, however, it is uncomfortable to ask people these questions," Darko counters.

"I told you at the outset that some of my beliefs may uncomfortably challenge you," Ned replies, "and here's a case where you're being challenged. My standard is simple. Prognosis without diagnosis is malpractice; therefore, I am unable to proceed with my presentation without the complete disclosure of the personal financial information of my clients. Once again, this is a matter of choice."

"What choice is that?" Darko asks.

"In this case, your choice is to ask them their personal financial information and fulfill your obligation, or choose to commit malpractice. Remember, these are just my standards, not the industry's standards, but I believe that when your standards exceed those in the industry, greater success follows. Exceeding standards helps you stand out from all the competitors and it is what the clients want."

"I guess I'll have to do this in all of my presentations from this point forward," Darko states.

"There is no guess work," Ned corrects him. "If your choice is to adopt my declaration of intent, then you'll have to follow the principles. Diagnosing my clients' exposures to the four financial perils is the core to fulfilling my obligation. As set forth in my declaration of intent, I am able to demonstrate my absolute competence as an insurance advisor during this part of the discussion. Diagnosing my clients' financial risks makes it clear why they need to buy insurance and demonstrates its importance to their financial well-being. I find that my clients appreciate my candor as well as my direct approach.

"The clients I want to do business with will consider their insurance a weighty matter," he continues. "They will consider their insurance to be their absolute financial foundation and will look to me as their advisor. Therefore, they will willingly divulge all of their financial information. They recognize that I am a competent, ethical insurance professional and that I am acting in their best interest," Ned finishes.

"Will they recognize that you love your clients?" Darko jokes.

Realizing it is a joke, but sensing the truth in it, Ned replies, "Yes. Darko, they will sense the love I have for all my clients."

"It is simple," Tony adds. "You must know all their financial information. You can't assume or guess anything."

"Once again, these are far too weighty of matters to assume or guess your clients' financial situation," Ned repeats. "You cannot implement a sound insurance buying strategy without knowledge. You must do your homework, prepare, and educate yourself so that you may assist your clients in transferring the insurmountable risk they face. It is a critical endeavor to transfer this daily risk."

"I believe we've got it. Prognosis without diagnosis is malpractice. I will adopt this standard," Tony says.

"I'm on board as well," Darko says.

"Excellent," Ned says. "This edict must become indelible because it is a heart and soul commitment, a pledge, the real crux of my belief system."

Ned pauses while Darko interjects some more of his humor, "Tony, I feel another one of his sermons coming."

They all laugh when Tony's eyes get wider in mock fear.

Undaunted, Ned continues, "Conscience is *the faculty of recognizing the distinction between right and wrong in regard to one's own conduct.* This is a very succinct definition, it is not vague, and neither should what we do for our clients be vague. If I don't know my client's complete financial condition, then I can't proceed. If I proceed without this information, then what I am doing is absolutely wrong. I can never compromise this edict. Never."

"I will have to admit that this has challenged me in the past," Darko says.

"Darko, once again, my beliefs and convictions may uncomfortably challenge you," Ned says.

"These tenets and principles are, I believe, of the highest standards. My ultimate goal on this trip has always been, and always will be, to awaken your conscience by stimulating and unleashing it so you will be able to fulfill your dreams and purpose. If I ignore my conscience—if prognosis ever precedes diagnosis at any time—then I am committing malpractice. This is the difference between right and wrong. This principle defines my conscientious standards for transferring and managing my clients' risk," Ned stops.

"Your definition of conscience is sinking deeper into mine," Darko admits. "My job, I now understand with clarity, is to assist my clients in always buying the right insurance. What scares me is that many of the clients I have today are not suitably protected against the perils they face and lack an insurance buying strategy. What do I tell these people?"

"Darko, these people represent your greatest opportunity," Ned replies. "You need to call them and invite them into your office for a comprehensive insurance review designed to transfer their insurmountable risk. Then you provide them with an insurance buying strategy that considers their insurance protection to be their financial foundation. It will protect them against financial ruin."

"What do I tell them about the bad advice that I have given them in the past?" Darko asks.

"You must be candid and direct," Ned says. "You tell them that you have come to understand a better strategy for purchasing their insurance. You tell them that this method will be in their best interest and, in most cases, they will respond to you with enthusiasm and interest."

"A clear conscience is definitely what I'm looking for in life," Tony offers.

"Conscience is universal," Ned confirms. "It is a natural occurring phenomenon that, I believe, is wired inherently into the human spirit. I believe we are all born with a clear, concise conscience.

"Ego conflicts with one's conscience at times, however," he continues. "Ego is selfish and tyrannical. It focuses merely on the individual's own survival and enhancement, while conscience elevates ego to a group mentality. Conscience concentrates on the greater good."

"My ego has been crushing my conscience," Darko admits. "My heightened conscience has caused me to discern that your beliefs and principles are not at all threatening. I realize now that you are only helping Tony and me."

"In review, we started by practicing the delivery of our declaration of intent," Ned begins. "You both gave excellent examples of how you will deliver, from the heart, your positioning statement to your clients from this day forward. You did not stumble or recite. You both sounded genuine. Then we prepared for the ethical consideration of conscience. The reason for this is that I sensed you both had already made your choices.

"Over time, I have realized that the discussion of conscience and the true search for the answer is a threat to one's ego, something that gets left behind when there is a heightened sense of purpose. I believe this heightened sense of purpose comes with understanding of why—logically and ethically—people need to buy insurance. This all comes from a defined and conscientious mission statement.

"If you intend to be an insurance advisor, then you must accept the responsibility of transferring and managing your clients' risks, even taking the worst-case scenario into account," he continues.

"This reality can be examined through the four financial perils. These lay the groundwork for a sound buying strategy and examination of consequential and inconsequential coverage. Finally, understanding that prognosis without diagnosis is malpractice, we are able to satisfy our innate conscience," Ned pauses to point out the upcoming turn to the conference. He takes the moment before arrival to whet Tony's and Darko's appetites for what is to come.

"Now that we have discussed the *why*, we can move onto the *how*," he says.

After a pause from Ned, Tony exposes his conscience, "I agree with everything you have said to this point, Ned. I will have to admit that this last edict of the declaration of intent has rekindled my conscience and awakened my spirit. My conscience has been awakened because you have taught me why people and families need to buy insurance. I accept this responsibility and understand how to raise my level of competence so that I will be accountable for all my actions."

Darko's agreement is expressed, "Tony, you have already communicated my sentiments. I am ready to forge ahead."

The men exit the car and enter the conference with open minds. They are eager to use their new knowledge when speaking to other agents at the conference, but also anxiously await the remainder of Ned's teachings after the weekend is over.

Chapter 7 Summary

- This chapter discusses the fifth principle of the declaration of intent: *We diagnose [our clients'] exposure to the four financial perils and then we help them obtain suitable coverage.*
- Prognosis without diagnosis is malpractice.
- In order to diagnose your client's exposure to the perils, they must provide you with their personal financial information including combined family income.
- Once you have obtained your client's financial information, you can design an insurance buying strategy for them to transfer the insurmountable financial risk of the perils associated with a worst-case scenario.
- As an insurance advisor, let your conscience guide you. Your conscience benefits you and your client, whereas your ego is tyrannical and only concerned with the selfish survival of you at the expense of others.

CHAPTER 8

FACE-TO-FACE

As the conference ends, there is a merging of several forces, new and old. Darko and Tony have had the opportunity to weigh and compare all the information Ned has given them. Ned was sure to give them lots of time during the conference to digest the information he presented and is now, for the first time since their arrival, reconvening with them. He can see by their smiles and enthusiasm that they are even more resolved to adopt his ways, which have touched and inspired their deepest conscience.

"You know what, Ned? I was so moved by your explanation and expansion on the idea of conscience that I am considering refraining from any cutting humor, at least for the duration of our drive home," Darko offers.

"But, you promised on the way here that you would always grace me with your witty quips," Ned says.

"Since I promised, I guess I will have to follow my conscience and jab you at my every chance," Darko says. "We've dried up these couple of days, do shower us again with your enlightenment, Ned."

"Yeah, don't we have one more principle from the declaration of intent to cover?" Tony joins in. "Let's get started learning how to apply everything you told us on the way here."

"All right, since you brought it up, Tony, would you please read the final principle?" Ned asks.

We conduct a face-to-face meeting with our clients and prospects to ensure our mission is accomplished.

"Sounds like a short discussion to me," Darko says. "You have to go eyeball-to-eyeball. Everyone knows that, but something tells me, with your wind, this discussion may be our longest yet."

"Darko, I will only spend the amount of time discussing the personal interview that is required for you to understand its value," Ned smiles. "If you'll come around as fast as Tony, I won't have to talk so much."

"I already meet all of my clients in person," Tony says confidently. "This tenet will be easy for me to adopt."

"Excellent, Tony," Ned says. "Hopefully, this discussion will impress masterful communication of your ideas and strategies while meeting in person."

"I hope to demonstrate that what you say and how you act will be more critical to your success and freedom than any other element of your business," he continues.

"The face-to-face interview is your time to shine and is integral to your personal survival as well as that of our profession. A face-to-face interview turns a numbers game into a people game. I believe we are engaged in a people business first and foremost; risk management should always be about the client," Ned says.

"Is this irrefutable?" Tony jokingly interjects before Ned has the chance to say it. Ned smiles and nods.

"You always hear people refer to insurance as a numbers game," Darko adds. "I heard that a lot this week. The advice was that the more appointments you have, the more money you'll make."

"What you just said, Darko, is only half the truth," Ned responds. "I believe, if you follow the tenets and principles of our conscience-laden declaration of intent, you will make it a people game first and, as a result, your numbers and compensation will follow commensurate to your skill level and ability to demonstrate overall competence."

"I understand what you're saying," Tony declares. "It is less about the number of appointments and more about quality appointments that better set you up for chances of success."

"Exactly," Ned says. "The better your performance, the better your results. Early on in my career it would take four appointments to make one sale. Today, most appointments lead to a sale. The declaration of intent will allow you to make more significant sales, more often."

"Going three for four is a lot more fun than going one for four," Darko says.

"You will wear yourself out," Ned starts, "going one for four all of the time. I will guarantee that discussing the four perils of insurance, consequential insurance coverage, and the worst-case scenario will improve your results. I believe you must become expert at the face-to-face interview, and the only way to become expert is to do it over and over again."

"I will admit that I am worn out," Darko says. "The first five years, when I was building my agency from the ground up, were new and exciting. The last three years, though, have been unnerving as well as exhausting. I've reached a plateau of burnout."

"Plateaus are blinding and debilitating," Ned says. "In a reaction to escape one of my debilitating plateaus, I developed my significant declaration of intent. You have to always grow in order to have a healthy agency, and you won't be able to grow if you don't know what to say and how to say it. That is why implementing my philosophy and delivering it in the personal interview is mandatory."

"I can't wait to get back to the office to implement your teachings and practice them," Tony says.

"Good, Tony," Ned commends. "I guarantee that your results will definitely improve. With all due respect, you and Darko have been engaged in the marketing of insurance and not the practice of insurance.

"An insurance advisor must practice his craft of advising through personal meetings with his clients and prospects. All parties must be present in order to fulfill your promise. You can't complete a comprehensive insurance review unless all interested parties are present and engaged in the process."

"But what about the situation where…" Darko begins to ask when Ned interrupts.

"There are no situations. There are no circumstances where you should deviate from this directive."

"The only review that you may do over the phone is with an existing client living outside of our immediate area who understands and subscribes to your philosophies. Initially, a new client or prospect must absolutely go through our comprehensive insurance presentation. Any exception to this edict I consider to be malpractice," Ned finishes.

"I tell people that this is the difference between buying face-to-face as to over the phone or via the internet," Tony says.

"Not exactly," Ned replies. "When it comes to buying the wrong insurance, there is no difference between buying insurance over the internet or through a 1-800 company.

"Tony, you need to start telling people the difference between you and all the competition is that you are a trusted insurance advisor capable of implementing a long-term insurance buying strategy. Start telling all prospects that you guarantee you can and will find a major gap in their insurance coverage.

"Many agents and companies are confused as to why they have lost significant business to these competitors," Ned continues. "They believe they have lost business due primarily to the price consideration. I argue that, in truth, they were not providing people with insurance buying strategies in the first place. The public has lost confidence in their traditional insurance agent and has, instead, turned to discounters.

"Frankly, insurance agents, as a collective group, have been failing to add value, and so, are valueless to their customers. Our challenge, as a group, is to raise our standards. We are in this together. If we don't make the transition from the traditional insurance agent to a trusted insurance advisor, our entire profession will be at even greater risk," Ned stops.

"You don't seem to have a lot of confidence in today's insurance agent," Darko says.

"I am not criticizing our profession," Ned assures him. "I am, however, providing you with an honest and fair assessment of the condition of our profession. Few agents are engaged in the practice of risk management; rather, they market insurance.

"They don't conduct comprehensive insurance reviews with their clients because they either don't have the time or, in most cases, the know-how. In fact, most agents, like most small business owners, are enslaved to their businesses and are not even aware of their condition. They are more concerned with what other carriers are doing than what they themselves are doing.

"You cannot aspire to be a trusted insurance advisor unless you are wholly committed to the comprehensive insurance review," Ned says. "It is the only way to fulfill our declaration of intent."

"I admit that, in the back of my mind, I have been trying to figure out how to take your information and tweak it to work for me in my situation," Darko says. "You have made it clear to me that my situation is not unique to me; the situation is universal. I now realize that I must adopt your philosophy in whole, there are no shortcuts."

"Thank you, Darko," Ned says. "You are starting to come around. Why do you think that is?"

"You are being so direct and candid with me that it is making sense. I now understand your teachings," Darko answers.

"Exactly," Ned replies. "This is how you should communicate with your clients, but you often hear people use the expression 'soft sell.' The whole idea behind this is ludicrous. Insurance is one's financial foundation. Soft-selling has had damaging effects on our profession. There is no soft selling in my operation. Soft selling is insincere and a form of incompetence. Clients appreciate direct communication.

"If my clients have gaps in their insurance coverage or lack an insurance buying strategy, I must tell them about their current state of affairs," he continues. "I cannot be apologetic or soft in my approach. I have conducted countless interviews using my direct approach and nearly all people respond in like fashion.

"Consider this," Ned says. "If you knew a tsunami was imminent, would you go up to people on the beach and soft sell them on this reality?"

"Of course not, most people would almost be hysterical when explaining the impending danger, and tell everyone to retreat to higher ground immediately," Tony jumps in enthusiastically.

"Well, I believe that I must warn my clients about their potential financial ruin with this same sense of urgency," Ned implores.

"I appreciate your candor," Darko says. "I now understand that I must always be direct with my clients. I understand that is what my clients want me to do for them."

"Understand that I am not advocating hard selling your clients either," Ned clarifies. "Rather, you should be direct with a combination of thoughtfulness and eloquence. Deliver your message with a clear and concise conscience. People appreciate this approach."

"Most of the people you meet with have legitimate concerns about their insurance, or they wouldn't be meeting you in the first place," Ned says. "I know that when I go to see my doctor, lawyer, accountant, or any professional for that matter, I want to be spoken to directly and truthfully so I can attempt to solve my problem.

"To that same degree, a person's financial future is far too important to walk softly around," he impresses.

"Wow, you don't mess around one bit," Tony realizes. "You get straight to the business at hand, don't you?"

"I firmly believe I have to get to the point," Ned says. "I can't predict when the next earthquake is going to occur, when the next hurricane is going to happen, or when one of my clients is going to suffer a fatality. These truths and realities force me to explain the legitimate financial concerns my client should consider; they force me to follow the principles of my declaration of intent at all times."

"Let's say I am meeting with somebody to discuss their auto insurance renewal and their home insurance expires later in the year. How do I handle this situation?" Tony asks.

"First of all, Tony, your appointments will not be to discuss one particular line of insurance anymore," Ned reminds him. "Remember, insurance is one product, one advisor, and one solution."

"Adopting this new approach allows you to avoid the pitfalls of the so-called apologetic cross sell. Your interview lays out your entire mission clearly and concisely. You'll promise your prospects that you will be able to find significant to reckless gaps in their insurance portfolio or prove they lack a sound insurance buying strategy. After completing your diagnosis, most clients will find your prognosis to be irrefutable and this confidence will give you the candor you need," he answers.

"What do you do about multiple expiration dates?" Tony rephrases his question.

"I write most of my clients' homeowner's insurance first, then gather their expiration dates," Darko says. "I get back to them prior to their next renewal."

"My philosophy is that a person's insurance should expire the day they find out how grossly under-insured their current agent or company has left them," Ned advances.

"For instance, let's assume you write the home first without doing a comprehensive insurance review, and then, using Darko's approach, apologetically get back to them to discuss their auto insurance at its so-called renewal or expiration date. Let's assume, like most people, they are grossly under-insured in either the bodily injury section or the uninsured motorist section. While they wait for their renewal date to remedy this grave situation, the declaration of intent is being violated. Waiting for the renewal tells the client that you lack the conviction that you professed to have during your mission statement," he finishes.

"What about their earned premium?" Darko asks. "I think switching midterm can lead to real problems."

"Earned premium is inconsequential and switching midterm will avoid the consequential problem someone will face if they are grossly under-insured and suffer a significant loss," Ned replies.

"We buy insurance because we don't know what the future holds. I train my agents that honoring expiration dates is a direct violation of the mission statement."

Ned pauses because he can see a comment brewing under the surface. Darko's quietness lifts as he comes to an understanding.

"This does challenge me; however, I get your point. In order to be an advisor, you must be definitive. Clients recognize and respect definitive answers and solutions."

"You are really starting to absorb and embrace the logic behind my beliefs," Ned says, "and I hope you understand that it is illogical to continue buying inadequate insurance for any period of time. If the boat is sinking, you must act logically or you will drown. The tough part that lies ahead for you will be putting these teachings into practice."

"This all makes complete sense to me," Tony says. "I can see how it will save me time and will be in the best interest of my clients."

"I agree as well," Darko chimes in, "but I would like some more clarification. If after diagnosing your clients' exposure you find they have suitable consequential coverage in place, would it be okay then to write the coverage at their renewal date?"

"Good question, Darko," Ned says. "The answer is yes. As long as the people have the suitable consequential coverage in place, then it would be appropriate to wait for the renewal."

"I understand there are two types of reviews," Tony begins, "the new client review and the existing client review. What is the difference between these two interviews?"

"The intent is the same in both interviews," Ned responds, "to follow the principles set forth in the declaration of intent. The difference lies in the amount of time each interview takes to complete.

"A new client review takes more time because you will be overhauling their entire insurance program and exposing the inadequacies of their existing program. It will be the most important presentation you make to your client because you will build a lifetime of trust.

"After securing this, your future reviews with this client will be short and concise because your client will already have bought into your philosophy. The new client presentation will take more careful explanation because this is the time that you'll be called upon to demonstrate your distinct advantage over their previous company or agent.

"A stellar performance in your initial meeting will set the tone for the entire relationship. A sub-par performance will most often lead you into a contentious business relationship; therefore, it is obvious that you would want to start your business relationship by delivering a stellar presentation. You want to be masterful, and the only way to become masterful is to practice," he finishes.

"How do you practice?" Tony asks.

"Your practice will start with the delivery of the declaration of intent. I recommend you practice this delivery on your family and friends. Darko, I recommend that when you sing in the shower, you start to sing the declaration of intent," Ned impresses.

"How do you know that I sing in the shower every morning?" Darko asks.

"Everybody knows that you sing in the shower, we could hear you down the hall at the conference," Ned chuckles. "And everybody knows deep down that their insurance has more than likely been mishandled in the past. Most people make their insurance premium payments with some reluctance because they are not certain that their insurance program will be adequate in the time of dire need.

"A comprehensive insurance review following the principles of our declaration is the only way to provide clients with the peace of mind they deserve" Ned continues. "The review makes insurance one single product.

"Unless you have examined all the financial risks, you cannot call yourself an advisor or consider yourself a risk manager.

"In order to do this, you must meet your client face-to-face and discuss all of their insurance. The face-to-face interview is the only way I am able to build absolute trust; therefore, the face-to-face interview must be a masterful presentation. It allows your clients to purchase your competent advice and illustrates that the price of insurance is of little significance. It is far better to have an advisor who works in their best interests.

"People deserve more than our industry has been providing its so-called precious customers in the past," he declares.

"You are right, the insurance industry's clients deserve more," Darko contributes. "I can admit almost all of the people I have met with have not had the proper insurance in place prior to our meeting and after, they still do not have the right insurance in place."

"On the other hand, in the existing client interview, you are fine tuning an already-sound strategy," Ned says. "For instance, you may be adding a vehicle and, at that time, you may need to increase liability limits or rewrite their life insurance to a larger policy. You will be, in essence, tinkering with an already sound and significant program."

"I now understand how I am going to approach my existing clients who need a complete overhaul of their insurance program," Darko says. "I will meet with them and tell them that I have found the best-known method for suitably placing their insurance and it will be in their best interest to meet with me as soon as possible."

"Yes, Darko," Ned responds. "I would recommend meeting with all your existing clients and treating these reviews as if they were new client reviews. The adoption of the declaration of intent into your agency will provide you with an opportunity to act as an advisor who will be able to significantly improve your agency's revenues. Most importantly, acting as an insurance advisor, you will be able to provide your clients with the proper and suitable coverage."

"I believe we've got it. You must be committed to the face-to-face interview. There is no other way," Darko says.

Ned points the way to an exit so they can stop for lunch. With the bulk of their discussion haven taken place on the way to the conference, the men now joke and take time to enjoy the drive and their choices. Ned knows there will be plenty of time to practice the face-to-face interview during the remainder of their car ride.

Chapter 8 Summary

- This chapter discusses the sixth, and final, principle of the declaration of intent: ***We conduct a face to face meeting with our clients and prospects to ensure our mission is accomplished.***

- Insurance is usually seen as a numbers game, and instead it should be a people's game. Face to face meetings ensure risk management stays a people's game. The face to face meeting between the advisor and the client is the foundation of a trusting relationship.

- The quality of meetings is much more important than the quantity of meetings.

- It is imperative to conduct a comprehensive insurance review with your client to examine all of their risks, then recommend an effective insurance buying strategy for them. You must avoid soft selling, up-selling, and cross-selling schemes and instead become a trusted advisor for all of your client's insurance needs.

- Insurance should be viewed as one product, one solution, one advisor.

- Utilize the comprehensive insurance review for both new clients and existing clients.

"Collaboration and cooperation will beat competition every time."

- Gail Lynne Goodwin

Chapter 9

THE FOUR PERILS AND THE AUTO POLICY
INTERVIEW PART I

Everyone has decided the trip home will provide plenty of time for practicing their new insurance approach. Tony is the first to express his enthusiasm.

"I'm excited the time has finally come for you to walk us through a comprehensive insurance presentation. I can't wait to see how you will guide us through the process by using your declaration of intent."

"I am a little scared to get started," Darko admits, "as I'm sure I will find out that my buyers beware approach has been worse than I thought it to be."

"Darko, don't worry so much because your heart has always been in the right place," Ned imparts.

"We have accomplished the most difficult task of putting your ego in check and elevating your conscience to a liberated level. Remember, following your conscience and leaving your ego at the door will be the key to freeing you from the shackles that bind you to your business. This profession is not about awards, compensation, nor prestige. It is about acting in the best interest of the hard-working people who willingly place their trust in you and the services you can provide."

"Understood," Darko says. "Will you proceed with our discussion and show us how we should conduct the presentation?"

"We spent considerable time discussing *why* you do what you do," Ned starts. "Now, a demonstration is in order to show you *how* to go about keeping your promise as advisor. For the purpose of this exercise, I will introduce you to a hypothetical family who, like most families, happens to be in dire need of a trusted insurance advisor," Ned says.

"I have an appointment on Tuesday with a close friend of mine named John," Tony chimes in. "I am already familiar with his and his wife, Lisa's, financial situation.

"I brought the file with me. I have my quotes, along with all of their existing declarations. Can we use his family as our example?"

Ned nods his head and accepts Tony's file.

"Before we get started, let me explain that any example we use will work," Ned says. "The declaration of intent is universal and works for almost all people in the marketplace. The one requirement for the declaration of intent to work is that you are dealing with a family or individual who is going forward financially. What I mean by that statement is that you must find clients who are concerned with their financial future. Can we assume that John is concerned about his family's financial future?"

"My friend is definitely concerned about his financial future," Tony says. "He has an income to protect, a home with equity, and is a very hard worker. He is also married and has two young children."

"Perfect," Ned says before starting his rendition of the declaration of intent. "It is imperative that in every new client comprehensive insurance presentation you require the prospect to bring all of his or her current insurance declarations to the meeting. Your presentation will not be as effective without the disclosure of their current insurance condition because it is designed to differentiate between your advice and the advice given by the previous insurance agent."

"I like the phrase 'current insurance condition,'" Darko contributes. "It implies that their current insurance portfolio is an unhealthy one."

"Good observation," Ned applauds him. "Tony and I are witnessing your personal metamorphosis.

"As for your observation, you are exactly right. I am using the word 'condition' because most of the people in the marketplace have unhealthy insurance portfolios. Their insurance condition needs healing."

"Not only that, but you've already taught us that nearly all the prospects we meet will be grossly under-insured in a critical area or will lack a commonsense insurance buying strategy," Tony, who is now behind the wheel, adds. "Ned, ready to roll?"

Ned begins the practice review.

"Thanks for coming in today, Tony. I appreciate the opportunity to examine the financial risks that you and your family face. I want you to understand that I don't want you to feel obligated to place your insurance with me based on our friendship. In the end, I want you to choose to do business with me only after I've demonstrated my overall competence and under the condition that it serves your best interest. Agreed?" Ned role-plays.

"Agreed," Tony says acting as his friend and prospective client.

"All right then," Ned continues. "I act as my clients' insurance advisor and handle most or all of their insurance. I find that most people I meet are over-insured in the areas where coverage is least needed and under-insured in the areas where coverage is most needed. The purpose of our meeting is to determine the proper and suitable coverage that you will need in the event of a worse-case scenario insurance loss.

"After diagnosing your exposure to the four financial perils you face on a day-to-day basis, I will help you implement a sound insurance buying strategy that will safeguard you against financial ruin.

"In order to accomplish what I have just communicated, I need to ask you some personal financial information," Ned completes the declaration of intent.

"That sounds fair to me," Tony says.

"What do you do, if you get resistance at this point?" Darko wonders aloud. "For instance, Tony's friend, John, says something like 'I don't know if I am willing to give you my personal financial information.'"

Ned swiftly replies, "In this case, I would respond by saying, 'Your insurance is your financial foundation and you can be sued for portions of your income and assets. If you were at fault in an accident where the limits of your insurance were not enough to satisfy a judgment handed down by a judge in a court proceeding, you would then be responsible for the excess liability. This is why I need to know your personal financial information.'"

"Excellent answer, please proceed," Darko says impressed by the simplicity of confidence imbued by the declaration of intent.

"At this point, I would ask John what his and Lisa's annual income is and the makeup of their assets."

Ned then proceeds with the role-play by asking Tony, "What is your combined family income?"

Acting as John, Tony answers, "Our combined income this past year was $100,000."

"How much of the income was yours and how much was your wife's?" Ned asks.

"My salary was $75,000, and my wife made another $25,000 doing some part-time bookkeeping," Tony answers. "For the most part, she is home with our children."

"Excellent, now I need to know the amount of equity you have in your home," Ned says.

"We have about $250,000 in equity in our home," Tony answers.

"What is the loan balance on your mortgage?" Ned asks.

"I would estimate it to be $195,000."

"Do you have any other real estate assets?"

"My wife has a third interest with her siblings in a condominium in Arizona. I would estimate her share of equity would be approximately $40, 000," Tony says.

"Next I will need to know about your cash and investments," Ned probes. "How much do you have in liquid savings?"

"We usually keep about $5,000 in savings," Tony says.

"Do you have any stocks or other investments?" Ned asks.

"I have $40,000 in my 401(k) plan and we have an IRA. These accounts total, I believe, about $14, 000," Tony responds.

"Based on these figures you have approximately $650,000 at risk to a lawsuit. This is based on three times your annual income added to the rest of your assets. You will need to carry liability limits of $500,000 on your home and auto policies. You will also need to purchase an umbrella policy for an additional $1 million in coverage," Ned states.

"What is an umbrella policy, and is it expensive?" Tony recounts a question he has heard before.

"An umbrella is an excess liability policy that is designed to safeguard you against financial ruin," Ned says.

"Umbrella policies are very affordable. In fact, they offer more coverage per premium dollar than any other policy you will need to purchase and provide great security in the event of a catastrophic liability insurance claim," he explains.

Both Tony and Darko are impressed with the ease and speed with which Ned collected necessary information. It was, as Ned promised, seamless and efficient. They await Ned's continued presentation. Ned quickly reviews the assets and income of this prospect and moves on.

Ned first begins the comprehensive insurance presentation by discussing the auto insurance policy because it leads to a discussion of the four perils. All concepts of the insurance buying strategy Ned advocates are introduced during this discussion. He starts the dialogue by introducing the lawsuit exposure peril in the bodily injury and property damage section.

"Bodily injury and property damage are the first coverages found in your auto policy," he begins.

"Bodily injury and property damage cover you in the event there is an at-fault accident and bodily injury or property damage occurs. If you are under-insured in this area and are at fault in an accident where severe bodily injury or fatality occurs, you could be led to financial ruin. Therefore, you need to carry a suitable amount of insurance to cover this exposure. Any questions?"

Tony and Darko shake their head and Darko waves his hand in Ned's direction as if giving him the floor, "Please continue."

"The next area of coverage you need to be concerned with is your uninsured motorist and under-insured motorist coverage. This area of coverage covers you for any bodily injury or fatality you may suffer if you are involved in an accident where the other party has insufficient liability coverage to protect you against your loss," Ned says.

Tony interjects, acting as John, "I didn't realize uninsured motorist protected you under these circumstances."

"Yes, in fact, based on your clean driving record and your specific demographic, the greatest risk that you will face regarding automobile insurance is being in an accident where the other driver is at fault and he or she has insufficient coverage to protect you against the loss," Ned says. "Allow me to explain."

"Nationwide, approximately 20 percent of all drivers on the road are uninsured. We can assume a minimum of another 20 percent of the drivers found on the road are under-insured. That means 40 percent of all drivers that you pass on a daily basis will be either uninsured or under-insured," Ned says.

"Although worrisome, those figures seem to make sense," Tony says.

Ned continues to address Tony's question. "These 40 percent have twice the accident rate where severe bodily injury or a fatality occurs. Therefore, based on the statistics, you have an 80 percent chance that, if you're involved in an accident, it will be the other guy's fault and they will not have the adequate insurance in force to protect you against this loss.

"Since uninsured motorist provides coverage for pain, suffering, and loss of income due to an injury or a fatality, we will need to focus our attention on your critical need for this coverage.

"The greatest financial risk you face when you get behind the wheel is loss of income," Ned concludes. "We need to solve this problem.

"Consider: If you are at fault in an accident and cause severe bodily injury to another party and were under-insured at the time of the loss, you have the chance of overcoming this loss because you'll have the ability to earn income. However, if you are permanently disabled or suffer a fatality at the hands of an uninsured or under-insured motorist, and you are under-insured at the time of loss, you more than likely will have no chance of financial recovery."

"This all makes sense," Tony offers, as John, "however, it's starting to sound expensive."

"At the outset of our discussion, I mentioned that you would be more than likely over-insured in some areas that lack consequence and probably grossly under-insured in some areas of great consequence," Ned starts. "Bodily injury and uninsured motorist coverage on your auto policy are areas of greatest consequence. They are the real reasons for buying auto insurance.

"The next coverages that I will discuss on your auto policy are those of less consequence," Ned continues.

"My philosophy is that you should assume risk in these areas so that you are able to free up the dollars for more critical areas of coverage. You may be surprised when, more than likely, we will be able to deliver the coverage you need at a similar cost.

"Are you following me or would you like further explanation?" he asks.

"I believe I'm getting it," Tony answers.

"So, the next area of coverage that is available to you on an auto policy is medical payments. Do you currently have medical insurance?" Ned asks.

"Yes, my family has a comprehensive plan," Tony answers.

"Do you know what the deductible and out-of-pocket expense is on your major medical coverage?" Ned continues.

"I believe we have a zero deductible, 20 percent co-insurance, and our out-of-pocket exposure is something like, $6,000 per person," Tony says.

"What is your monthly premium?"

"My premium is around $1,600."

"I am certain that premium is a significant, monthly expenditure," Ned says. "We will discuss this a bit later. We may be able to help you come up with a better strategy for your medical insurance."

"I am all ears. Those medical premiums have been sending me to the cleaners for a long time now."

"Then, my advice would be to forgo medical payments on your auto policy since you have a major medical insurance policy in place for your entire family. By eliminating this coverage, we are avoiding a duplication of coverage and are freeing up some premium dollars. We will take these savings and use them to finance the coverages of greater consequence, specifically bodily injury and uninsured motorist coverage," Ned responds.

"Makes sense," the role-playing Tony agrees.

"Next we will discuss the physical damage section on your auto insurance," Ned continues. "There are two physical damage coverages. The first is your comprehensive coverage which provides protection against damage to your vehicle caused by anything other than a collision, like vandalism, theft and windshield replacement.

"I will recommend a $1,000 deductible with a glass buy back provision. This means that the deductible for your glass will only be $100. You definitely want to be able to see when you are driving. So if you crack your windshield and have this coverage, you will only be responsible for the first $100," Ned says.

"The next physical damage coverage is collision. Your collision coverage protects you against damage to your vehicle when you are involved in an at-fault accident. I will recommend that you carry a minimum of $1,000 deductible for this coverage," Ned says.

"I believe my deductible is only $500 with my current carrier," Tony interjects. "I am not sure I want to go any higher."

"The best strategy for buying insurance is to assume the maximum amount of risk that you can reasonably afford," Ned says. "I will demonstrate to you that it is more prudent to go with a higher deductible and take those savings to finance the coverage that really matters to you.

"Based on your current financial condition, a $1,000 deductible is the minimum you should purchase. A $1,000 loss would be a slight inconvenience, but in the bigger picture, there are significant savings that come by increasing your deductibles."

"Some people are really set on keeping their lower deductible," Darko contributes.

Ned takes a detour of the role-playing to address Darko's very real concern.

"You are correct, Darko. But, if you can logically explain the merits of assuming additional risk and show them the money they save in premiums when they switch from a $500 deductible to a $1,000 deductible, people will change their attitudes.

"In addition, going with a higher deductible will help them avoid turning in small claims. I explain to my clients that their insurance record is critical to their overall costs. The more claims they have on their record, the more they'll have to pay.

"I tell people their insurance is for catastrophic losses and carrying a low deductible is an enticement to turning in a claim. Low deductibles are a shortsighted approach. You simply show the client the significant long-term savings they will receive by assuming more risk on the lower end," he says.

"Remember, the client's responsibility is to assume a reasonable amount of risk so that they will be able to transfer their overwhelming risk to an insurance company," Ned goes on.

"Once again, your clients need bodily injury and uninsured motorist coverage. They don't need inconsequential medical payments, comprehensive and collision, or towing and rental car coverage.

"They need the deep pockets of insurance that provide financial protection. In this instance, there is only a $500 difference in the deductible. That $500 difference is inconsequential. Insurance is for the bigger things," Ned finishes.

"Wow, auto insurance really *is* all about bodily injury and uninsured motorist," Tony exalts.

"Yes, Tony," Ned affirms. "It's about perils and consequences."

"You really do have insurance figured out, don't you Ned?" Darko says admiringly.

"Darko, I figured out long ago there are no secrets," Ned reminds him. "There is no trickery; there are only truths and realities. The truth is that insurance is an artistic, mathematical equation. The reality is that being accountable to my clients is an awesome responsibility and I must be prepared to assume this responsibility.

"Tony's friend, John, could be involved in a serious accident the very next time he steps into his vehicle," he relates. "The truth is, Tony must do his very best to provide the financial security that his friend and family may need.

"Calamity does not discriminate, it doesn't know gender, race, creed or social status. It can come at any time or place to anyone. Tony's mission—his obligation—will be to prepare his friend for the worst case scenario," Ned stops.

"Well spoken," Darko applauds.

"Thank you, Darko," Ned smiles, recognizing Darko's agreeable side has peeked out on this return trip home. He then continues by reviewing the discussion they have just completed.

"Auto insurance discussions unveil the complete insurance buying strategy. In our mock comprehensive insurance review with Tony's friend, we were able to expose the significant need for bodily injury and uninsured motorist. This demonstrated that the lawsuit exposure peril and the loss of income peril are the real concerns that we must consider.

"The discussion introduced the medical insurance peril, and it exposed the property peril as well. The property peril was shown to be the least significant of the four perils. It demonstrated that this is the area where people should assume more risk," Ned explains.

"I remember our discussion of the four perils of the auto policy on the ride to the conference," Tony says. "I will admit I didn't grasp its significance, but I think after watching it unfold, I get it now."

"Remember, we are not selling auto policies, home policies, medical policies or life insurance policies," Ned impresses. "We are advising our clients on concepts and strategies designed to safeguard a family or individual from financial ruin."

"The fact that the four perils are found in the auto policy alone allows you to explain your insurance buying strategy and entire belief system in one very simple, methodical discussion. When we move on in the interview with Tony acting as his friend, we will discuss his home, medical, and, finally, life insurance."

"I've said it before and I'll say it again," Darko proclaims, "I can't wait to get to the life insurance discussion."

"Darko, we have already discussed their life insurance needs," Ned assures him. "Life insurance falls in the loss of income peril. You see, that is the beauty of the four perils and the auto policy. You will already have convinced your client about their life insurance needs when you discussed the uninsured motorist. Also, you will use the same philosophy that we used with the comprehensive and collision discussion when you discuss home insurance.

"The four perils of insurance approach makes your presentations seamless. You will no longer become anxious transitioning from product to product because there will be no transitions. There is only ***one product, one advisor, and one solution.***"

Darko and Tony are beginning to realize and believe that insurance *is* one singular financial product. The lessons they learned on the way to the conference are starting to make complete sense as they watch them unfold in the practice interview Ned is conducting. Both men are in eager anticipation to hear Ned complete the comprehensive insurance presentation.

Chapter 9 Summary

- The auto policy is a great place to start your comprehensive insurance review because people are required to have auto insurance both by their state and by their lender. Plus, the auto policy contains all four of the financial perils.

- The financial information you will need from your client before conducting the insurance review is: annual income, home equity, real estate assets, and cash and investments including stocks and bonds. This will help you determine what the client has at risk in a lawsuit. The lawsuit peril is contained in the bodily injury and property damage section of the auto policy.

- At-fault accidents where bodily injury and property damage occur could lead to financial ruin if under-insured in this area. You should determine the liability coverages needed in this area based on the client's annual income. You can supplement these coverages with an umbrella policy to insure against a worst case scenario.

- Uninsured or under-insured motorist coverage protects you when involved in an accident where the other driver has insufficient liability coverage to protect you against your loss.

- Medical payments are of less consequence especially if you have adequate medical insurance. You should advise clients to forego this coverage to avoid duplication of their current medical insurance, plus it frees up premium dollars for more important coverages.

- The two physical property damage coverages in an auto policy are comprehensive and collision, and these are also of less consequence.
    - **Comprehensive** covers damages to your vehicle caused by anything other than a collision (vandalism, theft, etc.). Recommend your clients carry a minimum $1,000 deductible with a ($100) glass buyback provision.

- ° **Collision** covers damages to your vehicle when you are involved in an at fault accident. Recommend that your clients carry a minimum $1000 deductible.
- Low deductibles are expensive (cost more premium), plus they lead to turning in more claims, which causes premiums to go up even more. High deductibles keep these expenses down which keeps premiums lower. This money can then be used to safeguard against insurmountable risks.

"A house is a home when it shelters the body and comforts the soul."

- Phillip Moffitt

CHAPTER 10

GIMME SHELTER
INTERVIEW PART II

Rolling easily from the auto insurance policy to homeowner's, Ned looks at Tony's and Darko's eager faces, happy to be able to give them the information they long to hear.

"In part one, we built our clients' foundation by explaining the insurance buying strategy. In part two of our discussion, we will discuss their home and umbrella, and provide them with the shelter they may need someday in the event of a financial crisis.

"When you discuss a person's home and umbrella coverage, you will expand the risk management approach established in the auto presentation. Remember, you cannot manage your client's financial future unless you examine all of the risks they face," Ned says.

"These are a lot of subjects to talk about," Tony postulates, "and I have been taught that you do not want to overwhelm people."

"Interesting," Ned raises one eyebrow at Tony. "Perhaps you want to underwhelm them?"

Tony and Darko exchange glances, realizing that Ned is going to go on another rant.

"What you just said, Tony, is taking the soft sell, apologetic approach," Ned explains.

"The soft-sell approach conveys you as your client's friend, the nice insurance agent who doesn't want to ruffle their feathers; the one who comes up with backdoor lingo in order to avoid speaking directly about things that matter."

"This is not the way of an advisor, but the way of someone who does not put the right insurance in place in times of need," he continues. "These are the ways of agents who cover over their inadequacies with flowers, get well cards, and of course, when they are exposed as being inadequate, will say, 'We are very sorry from the bottom of our collective hearts.'

"Tony, let me tell you something: you want to overwhelm your clients. You want to deluge your clients with today's truths and realities in order to fulfill the promise of our declaration of intent."

Speechlessness falls upon all in the car. Ned has expressed truth and everyone is letting it sink in. Finally, it is Darko who breaks the silence to defend Tony.

"Easy on the young feller, he is only relaying something he has been taught in the past."

Tony, revealing that he is more interested in truth than any injury to his ego responds, "That's okay, I have thick skin. I just learned something. There may be retribution for anything that comes out of my mouth."

"Exactly right," Ned says. "Those who search for truth take no offense. Learning to listen without taking it personally will help you as an advisor when your client makes an emotionally charged objection or opinion. Responding from your conscience prevents you from taking it personally, while leading with your ego can be paralyzing," Ned pauses to catch his breath and then proceeds.

"I believe you must overwhelm your clients with logical, rational solutions to their problems. Insurance is far too important of a purchase to tap dance around, you must rescue them from the incompetent insurance buying strategy that they are employing at the moment. The comprehensive insurance presentation does not take that much time. The more you practice the presentation, the faster and more convincing you will become.

"In fact, I have had people stop me five minutes into a presentation because they had heard enough to trust me. The confidence and knowledge expressed during the presentation makes people comfortable that I know what I am talking about. Rather than scaring people off, it helps clients realize just how poorly they are currently insured. Believe me, your clients want you to overwhelm them with reality," Ned imposes.

"I think people tell you that just because they want you to shut up," Darko kids.

"Maybe," Ned responds. "Either way, my position is if they choose to do business with me, then they will be in better hands than they were before.

"But, enough lecturing, are you now ready to roll with part two?"

Darko and Tony nod their heads in agreement.

"Picking up where we left off, I leave the auto discussion and go directly to their homeowner's insurance. Tony, are you ready to role-play as John again for the purpose of our discussion?" Ned asks.

"Aye, Aye, Captain," Tony says.

"Now, in your case, your home is your single largest investment," Ned begins. "You want to make certain that you can replace it if it is destroyed by a catastrophic event. I will first need to know the square footage of your house."

"Our house is a 1,800 square foot single-story house with an attached two car garage, which is I believe 500 square feet," answers Tony, acting as his friend and prospect.

"For the purpose of this discussion, we will assume that the reconstruction costs for this home will be $150 per square foot. We will calculate the square footage cost of the garage to be $100 per square foot. Based on the reconstruction costs in our area, we will need to insure your house for the amount of $320, 000," Ned states.

"Wow," Tony says, "I think we only have it insured for $225,000."

"After we are done with this discussion we will take a look at that," Ned comforts him. "Remember though, at the outset of our discussion I told you that you would more than likely be grossly under-insured in the areas where coverage is most needed. We have uncovered the first evidence of this common condition."

"I remember your specific words," Tony says.

"I also said that you would be over-insured where coverage is least needed," Ned continues. "I am sure we will find that you have a low deductible. I will advocate we increase your coverage to $320,000 and increase your deductible to a minimum of $2,500.

"Your dwelling coverage is a consequential component of your insurance protection. You need to be certain that you will be able to rebuild your house in the event of a total loss.

"In addition, you need to be certain that you have the proper building code upgrade coverage. Building code coverage provides protection against the increased cost of construction associated with building code changes. Gaps in coverage in this area can be very expensive and will lead to great frustration. We cannot leave you under-insured in this area.

"Have I left you with any questions?"

"No, I am following you," Tony responds. "You're making perfect sense."

"Excellent, let's move on to discuss the personal property coverage contained in your homeowner's policy," Ned continues. "Most people are surprised at the value of their personal property at the time of a total loss. We will make sure that you have the proper protection in this area of coverage.

"There are certain limitations of coverage on your personal property that we should discuss. For instance, your jewelry has limitations for theft. You also have limitations for guns and business property. You have the option to purchase additional coverage to increase these limitations. However, based on your current financial condition I would not recommend spending premium in these areas," Ned says.

"My wife's wedding ring is worth about $5,000, so what would be my limitation?" Tony asks.

"You would have $1,000 limitation for theft," Ned answers. "To insure your wife's wedding ring would cost approximately $125. I will advise you to save the premium in this area and use it to buy additional coverages you will need to satisfy more consequential needs in your insurance program. In addition, buying the coverage is a claim enticement.

"Frankly, you want to minimize your exposure to small claims. Turning in small claims will have an adverse effect on your future costs and, in some cases, lead to cancellation. I will advise you to assume the risk of small claims every time," he impresses.

"Understood," Tony says, once again role-playing the part of his friend and prospect.

"Good," Ned marches on. "Loss of use coverage is provided in your homeowner's insurance. Again, if you are involved in a total and complete homeowner loss, you will have to live somewhere else during the time your house is being rebuilt. Your mortgage payment will continue to be due in the event of a total loss, so you will need money to pay for the additional living expenses associated with your loss. I will advise you to purchase 24 months of coverage because in many cases it may take more than a year to rebuild your home."

"The next coverage of significant concern in relation to your homeowner's policy is your comprehensive personal liability coverage. Personal liability coverage protects you from non-intentional accidents you or a family member may cause. You'll need to purchase this coverage. Then, we will improve the limits of this coverage by installing an umbrella policy into your insurance portfolio," Ned finishes.

"We talked about the umbrella policy earlier. Would you please explain this policy in greater detail?" Tony asks.

"Of course Tony," Ned says. "As I said before, your umbrella liability policy will provide you with the additional liability limits you will need in order to protect your assets and future income from a lawsuit.

"We diagnosed your risk exposure to be $650,000. The maximum limit you will be able to purchase on your auto policy is $500,000. This would leave you with $150,000 of asset and future income exposure. Purchasing an umbrella policy will close this gap.

"The fact is, Tony, that you want more coverage than you have at risk because this coverage is consequential to your financial well-being. Being under-insured in this area is much too great of a risk for you to assume. As time goes by, your assets and income will grow, and in addition, your exposure will also grow. You simply can't afford to assume risk in the lawsuit exposure peril."

"I'm starting to understand," Tony contributes. "I don't want to lose my hard-earned dollars."

"Your umbrella policy will also include an endorsement that will increase your uninsured motorist coverage by an additional $1 million," Ned continues. "As we discussed earlier, your uninsured motorist protection is vital to your insurance portfolio. Self-insuring or underinsuring in this area is illogical."

Ned pauses before asking. "Can you see that your umbrella policy provides both of us with significant peace of mind?"

"Yes, it does seem to make sense for both of us," Tony says. "I am just afraid of the cost."

"I wouldn't worry too much," Ned reassures, "because I am near certain we will be able to offset the additional costs associated with improving your consequential coverage by the savings created through reduction or elimination of inconsequential costs currently burdening your portfolio.

"Once again, insurance is for catastrophic events, not inconvenient mishaps."

"I'm still interested in seeing the numbers," Tony says, as John.

"Of course," Ned says. "After all, risk management is all about numbers. To determine the proper and suitable coverage for you, I have taken all of your numbers—income, square footage, savings, and other financials—and I have either added or multiplied these figures to determine your exposure.

"Risk-management is a mathematical equation with a logical conclusion. My job is to design an insurance buying strategy that will eliminate your choices. In the end, all of my recommendations will be definitive," Ned pledges.

"That seems fair enough to me," Tony says.

"You have made a number of references to eliminating choices," Darko notes. "Can you please elaborate for us?"

Ned diverges momentarily for clarification.

"Of course," he says. "After diagnosing my client's exposure through a comprehensive insurance review, I eliminate my client's perceived choices. They provide me with all of their personal financial information, and I provide them with an irrefutable solution to their insurance buying problems. I determine the value of their home, their suitable need for health insurance, their exposure to a lawsuit, and their loss of income exposure, and then we place the suitable insurance for their unique situation.

"The answers and solutions are what they are. In the end, the only choice I will give my client is his mode of payment. Do they want to pay monthly, quarterly, or by electronic funds transfer? Believe it or not, these are the only choices your clients should have to make, and you should help them make these decisions as well," Ned finishes.

"I can see that we are eliminating the choices Tony's friend thinks he has to make," Darko says. "Really, he doesn't need choices, he needs a single solution and an insurance buying strategy designed to safeguard against financial ruin.

"By making the choice to conduct business in this manner, I will be able to assist my clients in eliminating a choice that could haunt them for years to come."

"Wow!" Ned praises him. "That was impressive. Deep down I have been hoping you would allow yourself to reach this understanding. After all, I have always known that you had the heart for it."

"Thank you very much, Ned," Darko responds. "That means a lot."

"Excellent, now, let's get back to the interview. Are you ready, Tony?" Ned asks.

"Ready," Tony affirms.

"Let's continue by providing an irrefutable insurance buying solution and help John eliminate his choices."

"Now that you have provided me with all of your personal financial information, I will explain the needed coverages for you and your family," Ned begins again, pretending that Tony is John. "These will safeguard you against financial ruin. I will start with your auto insurance.

"You will need to carry a bodily injury limit of $500,000 and a limit of $100,000 for your property damage liability. In addition, we will provide you with a limit of $500,000 on your uninsured motorist coverage. I will advise you to eliminate the inconsequential medical payments that are available to you. Do you follow me?" Ned asks.

"Yes, I am following you," Tony responds.

"Regarding your physical damage coverage that we discussed earlier, I will advise you to increase your deductibles to $1,000, both for comprehensive and collision. Any questions?" Ned asks again.

"No, you may proceed," Tony responds.

"We will now proceed to your homeowner's insurance. Based on construction costs for your area, as well as the size of home, I will advise you to insure your home for $320,000. You told me that you currently have your home insured for $225,000. I will advise you to carry a $2,500 deductible. Increasing your deductible will offset the increased cost to insure your home properly, and will also prevent you from turning in an inconsequential claim, which would have an adverse effect on your insurance record.

"Remember, your insurance record is vital to controlling your insurance costs. An insurance claim, in most cases, will result in a premium surcharge. This is a major reason that it makes sense for you to assume as much risk as possible. In your case, a $2,500 deductible is an appropriate assumption of risk," Ned finishes the homeowner's discussion.

"Did you include building code upgrades, my house's contents and all the other stuff we discussed earlier?" Tony asks.

"Yes, all of what I discussed will be part of the proposal," Ned answers before asking, "Are you ready to discuss your umbrella coverage?"

"I believe so," Tony says, as John.

"We have already touched on the subject of your umbrella coverage during our discussion," Ned says. "Let me start by saying your umbrella policy will be the core to protecting you from your lawsuit exposure and your uninsured motorist exposure. The umbrella policy is designed to provide you with the deep pockets that you may need some day to solve a serious problem.

"Tony, you have already proven to be on a path to success, and we don't want to impede the progress of that path. To ignore your exposure would be illogical. Your umbrella policy is mandatory. I will advise you to carry a $1 million limit, and we will endorse your uninsured motorist coverage for an additional $1 million," Ned says.

"Let's move on to discuss your health insurance. When we discussed your health insurance at the outset, you said you paid $1,600 in monthly premium?" Ned asks.

"That is correct, and I believe we have a PPO," Tony acts as his friend, John.

"Earlier in our discussion, you indicated that your out-of-pocket exposure was $6,000 for your family. Is that correct?" Ned asks.

"I believe so, however, I would have to look that up," Tony says.

"Do your wife or your kids have any pre-existing conditions, health problems, or any prescription medications?" Ned asks.

"First, you asked me about all of my personal financial information. Now you are prying into all my personal health information," Tony comments.

"In order to strategize about one of your greatest monthly expenditures, I need to know more personal information than most any other professionals working with you, but rest assured that all of your information is held in the strictest confidence. This discussion will never leave this room. That is my promise," Ned clarifies his position.

"All right then, the answer is that we are all very healthy," Tony responds. "I can't think of any pre-existing conditions we might have."

"Thank you," Ned says, "you have given me all the information I will need to examine your health insurance needs. We will need to meet at a later date in the presence of your wife to discuss this further. I will need to look at a synopsis of your current coverage before I can advise you on this matter."

"Would you like to set an appointment for next week sometime?" Tony asks.

"Before I set a follow up appointment, let's first examine your life insurance needs," Ned responds. "As we discussed in the uninsured motorist discussion, loss of income is your family's single greatest financial risk. Life insurance is designed to replace the income your family would lose upon your premature death."

"My belief is that any time I die will be untimely," Tony jokes, still role-playing.

"I know we all wish we could live forever, but this is not the case," Ned states. "You have significant life insurance needs and they must be addressed.

"So, Tony," Ned starts, "here's what we need to do. We will book an appointment for next week to meet with both you and your wife. I will need you to bring a copy of your health insurance and any life insurance policies you may already have. Do you currently carry life insurance on any of your family?"

"I think I have one year's annual salary at my job. I will find out for certain, though."

"Sounds great, Tony. We will set an appointment for a follow up to the health and life insurance discussion. I will take you into the next office and one of our agents, Liz, will collect your money and bind your coverage. I will also have Liz arrange a time for our next meeting," Ned finishes.

"Wait a second, Tony. You were too easy on him. You barely offered any resistance," Darko interrupts.

"I wasn't too easy on him," Tony counters. "His entire presentation made complete sense, and it was obvious that he was acting in an advisory capacity. Not once did Ned try to sell anything. I will have to admit that his presentation was rational and was, pardon the expression, irrefutable."

"Darko, when you start using this approach, you will find that you will receive less resistance than before," Ned points out. "People only offer resistance when they don't understand the benefit that you are offering. Objections most often are the result of a flawed presentation. Our presentation was not flawed. It was methodical, logical, and most importantly, had purpose.

"Tony's friend, John, wanted to do business with you in the first place. People meet with you hoping that their insurance buying situation will improve. The problem is that most agents meet their clients on the premise that they will save them money.

"Remember, you don't save money on insurance," he continues. "Insurance always costs your clients money. I only represent carriers that are dependable and offer significant consequential coverage because insurance is not a commodity. I have found that when you can explain to people the real reasons they need to buy insurance and how they need to do it, they will offer very little resistance.

"Believe me; my clients feel good about the money they spend on their insurance because I make them understand how important the products I provide are to their financial well-being," Ned finishes.

"I never considered the fact that people are meeting with me with the intention of making a change," Darko admits. "My mindset has always been 'from what angle do I approach each client?' For instance, what are their hot buttons or what conversations should I avoid. Our time together has taught me that there are no angles or hot buttons, and there are no conversations to be avoided. Hot buttons are a frivolous waste of time.

"Your declaration of intent will allow me to hit things head-on and help me address the core issues," Darko continues. "I must relinquish my propensity to engage in peripheral discussions, such as their payment mode, renewal date, or how far they drive their car to work. These factors, I realize now, are inconsequential to my position.

"The fact is I must always view my clients' insurance as their financial foundation and myself as a trusted insurance advisor. I have learned that there is no other way for me to respond to these teachings. I must begin to take a stand!"

"Once again, well-spoken and understood," Ned says. "I feel both of you are on your way to making the right choices. I advise we set up a game plan. We are getting close to home, and we still have work ahead of us.

"My suggestion is that we discuss the objections and problems you face, as well as, the ones you need to anticipate," he says. "You may have questions regarding the role-play interview that we have just completed. We will finish our ride with this discussion and, then, may I suggest we meet at my office on Saturday morning at 9 a.m. to complete the follow-up life and health presentation."

"We are almost home? The ride home flew by!" Tony gushes, reflecting on how interesting the discussion was and how his enthusiasm enlivened something he normal hates to do. He smiles thinking about how much more so this enthusiasm will add to the joy of his profession.

"Focus, Tony," Darko interjects realizing that Tony is on a mental hiatus.

"Sorry, Saturday morning works for me," Tony returns.

"That will do for me, as well." Darko affirms.

"Okay then, please fire away your questions," Ned directs.

"More for clarification, your strategy for a new client will be to complete the comprehensive presentation, bind the coverage for their casualty insurance, and then set up a follow-up for their life and health insurance. Am I right?" Tony asks.

"This would be ideal," Ned answers. "You have the authority to bind their property and casualty insurance, so this is your most immediate concern. Casualty insurance gives you the ability to help your clients immediately. Remember, if your clients are grossly under-insured, you need to act with urgency. Since you are not able to bind health and life insurance, you set up a follow-up appointment to meet with both spouses.

"In addition, when you take on a new client, you are often overhauling their entire insurance portfolio. I tell my clients that overhauling their insurance will take time and effort from both parties. The initial overhaul takes the most work and time, but it is worth it."

"When you have all of the client's business, I find it is easier to service them," Darko adds.

"The real question you need answered is: why should my clients and prospects do business with me?" Ned says. "If you are unable to answer this question, you will reduce your proposal to a question of price.

"You must answer this question, not only for yourself, but for your clients. They need to know and understand why you aren't playing the best price game and that refusing to do so is in their best interests. Too many agents are shackled by this maddening game and don't seem to want to leave it behind.

"Marketing sends the message that price matters most. Never forget you are not selling price but, as an advisor, you are selling protection. In order to do so, you must prepare, educate and commit yourself. You'll be surprised at the number of people who are willing to pay more for their insurance once they understand their irrefutable needs," Ned stops.

"I can see there is more to it than the adage: sell on price—lose on price," Darko comments. "The price will be what it will be.

"Until this lesson I didn't understand the real dynamics and components of risk transfer and management. I can't concern myself with price anymore because some of my clients need more coverage. I realize I am going to have to go back to these clients and use logic to convince them of their real needs.

"I also realize that part of the problem has been that I haven't had the skill level to convince my clients," Darko continues. "People haven't bought the proper insurance from me because I haven't been able to explain why they need it. Some of my clients have the proper worst-case scenario protection because, for whatever reason, they trusted me. Although, when I think about it, even in these cases I haven't sold them the suitable insurance.

"I am guilty of selling a significant amount of inconsequential coverage. I have many customers who have rental car coverage and medical payments but don't have umbrella or life insurance policies. I knew they needed these policies, but I wasn't able to offer them an irrefutable solution.

"The bottom line is that I haven't been really and truly accountable for my actions. If one of my grossly under-insured clients was involved in a serious accident and I haven't done my best to assist them in transferring that risk, then my acts have been negligent," Darko finishes.

Ned nods approvingly and then ties in the conversation to the values of most people.

"I want my clients to buy value from my agency because they know we are personally interested in protecting them. Using this approach I am able to free them from the distrust created by the buyer beware approach. I don't believe it is my client's responsibility to be a savvy buyer; I believe it is my responsibility to be a competent and capable provider of insurance protection. In the end, I want my clients and their families to be riding on my advice," Ned explains.

"You are right," Darko says. "Our clients deserve to be riding on our advice. The four perils and the consequential and inconsequential view make insurance one single product, with one solution. I can see, when you implement the insurance buying strategy through these principles, the price consideration will diminish. For the most part, the major companies' prices are going to fall within 10 to 20 percent of one another at any given time. I believe you could be in the 20 percent higher category and still provide your customer with a distinct advantage."

"Implementing the insurance buying strategy to your clients' portfolio will improve their current insurance condition," Ned says. "By eliminating and reducing your client's exposure to the inconsequential coverages, you will be able to deliver the coverages of consequence at, oftentimes, a similar to lower cost. Either way, the price doesn't matter.

"I will say, however, there are cases where a client will make price his or her only consideration," Ned adds. "Frankly, these are not the clients who you should elect to serve. Remember, not every client is a good client. If you deliver a command performance of your comprehensive insurance presentation and your client fails to respond, you have not failed, but, you may have succeeded in avoiding entrance into a risky business relationship.

"In the end, both you and the client should win," he clarifies. "You win because you've created a revenue stream that will fuel your agency. The client wins because, for the first time, they have bought the right insurance. One client will not make or break an agency, but one grossly under-insured situation can make or break an individual or family," Ned further imparts.

"Knowing that a single household is inconsequential revenue to any agency is an advantage because it helps me to be honest and provide an irrefutable insurance buying strategy," Darko contributes. "I am freed from the fear of losing a client and am able to better inform and help them. I can see my service as a favor to them. As you just said, one client will not make or break any agency, but one incompetent oversight can lead a family or individual to financial ruin. Making price a major consideration will lead me into an ethical dilemma."

"Upon the discovery of a grossly under-insured loss in a critical area, your clients will need to spend the additional money in order to solve their problem," Ned confirms what Darko has said. "Selling insurance on price is ignoring the inevitable downside.

"I believe our industry and profession has been damaged as well as impaired by turning insurance into a discussion about price. It denies our clients their moral right to buy the suitable insurance and gives them a false sense of comfort. Price causes insurance agents to have deceptive discussions that lend themselves to cheating and encourages fraudulent practice. Talks about cost lead to dissatisfaction, increased litigation, as well as, bad faith. Insurance is not about rating factors, discounts and payment plans, it is about truths and realities, perils and consequences. Discussing truths and realities, perils and consequences leads to satisfaction, goodwill, and decreased litigation.

"In the end, the 'cost of price' will cost many insurance agents their livelihood; however, the trusted insurance advisor of the knowledge age will thrive and prosper from his or her knowledge and acceptance of the 'cost of price'," Ned finishes just in time for them to pull into the office where they met to leave for the conference.

Again, Tony looks around in amazement that they have already found their way home. Enthusiasm and knowledge have made the path short and logical. Both Tony and Darko express gratitude to Ned for accompanying, and leading, their journey. They confirm their meeting on Saturday to discuss life and health insurance buying strategies.

Chapter 10 Summary

- In most cases, a client's home is their single largest investment.
- You need to recommend sufficient coverage for your client to be able to replace their home if destroyed by a catastrophic event.
- Components of your homeowner's policy include:
    - **Dwelling coverage**—calculate the square footage of your client's home and then determine the reconstruction costs to determine what coverage they need for their homeowner's policy.
    - **Building code coverage**— provides protection against increased costs of construction due to building code changes.
    - **Personal property coverage** – ensures the client has proper protection for the contents of their home within certain limits (for instance, jewelry, guns, etc.) with appropriate deductibles to keep premiums low and avoid frivolous claims
    - **Loss of use coverage** – covers the temporary living costs while the original home is being rebuilt. Recommend 24 months of coverage.
    - **Comprehensive personal liability coverage** – protects from non-intentional accidents caused by a client's family members. Clients need to purchase basic coverage here that we will improve upon with an umbrella policy.
- An umbrella policy provides clients with the additional liability limits to protect their assets and future income from a lawsuit. An umbrella policy is typically made in excess of a client's homeowner's and automobile insurance. Recommend that clients carry a $1 million limit plus an uninsured motorist endorsement for an additional $1 million.
- When transitioning to discuss health and life insurance:
    - First, gather basic health information from your client and assure them it will be held in the strictest confidence.

- ◦ Ask for their current health insurance coverages before you reconvene with them at a later time to finish this part of their insurance buying strategy.
  - ◦ Then move to life insurance: ask your client to provide copies of any life insurance policies they already have so you can review when you reconvene.
- Before you set an appointment to reconvene to finalize their health and life insurance applications, present your recommended insurance buying strategy to your client. This involves reviewing their current coverages and how they are under-insured where they most need insurance (consequential) and over-insured where they least need insurance (inconsequential). Then show your client your recommendations tailored to their individual needs that will protect them in the event of a worst-case scenario.
- Once they agree to this irrefutable strategy, bring them to your staff to collect their money and bind their coverage. Then schedule the follow up appointment to finish their health and life insurance application (and both spouses must be present). In the end, both you and the client should win. You win because you've created a revenue stream that will fuel your agency. The client wins because, for the first time, they have bought the right insurance. One client will not make or break an agency, but one grossly under-insured situation can make or break an individual or family.
- The real question you need answered is: why should my clients and prospects do business with me? Why is it in their self-serving interests and a clear advantage to them to place their trust, as well as, their insurance coverage with your agency? If you are unable to answer these questions, you will reduce your proposal to a question of price. They need to know and understand why you aren't playing the best price game and that refusing to do so is in their best interests.
- In the end, the 'cost of price' will cost many insurance agents their livelihood; however, the trusted insurance advisor of the knowledge age will thrive and prosper from his or her knowledge and acceptance of the 'cost of price.'

"The foundation of success in life is good health: that is the substratum fortune; it is also the basis of happiness. A person cannot accumulate a fortune very well when he is sick."

- P. T. Barnum

HEALTH AND CIRCUMSTANCE! INTERVIEW PART III

Saturday morning has arrived and Tony and Darko are eager to learn more of Ned's insights. The ride to and from the conference was a self-proclaimed cathartic experience, for both of Ned's new students.

Upon his return, Tony was able to convince his wife for the first time that his career decision would not be such a risk after all. He was able to make his wife start to believe that his new career choice was his best available option.

For Darko, the ride to the conference had overhauled his entire belief system. Darko came to realize that it takes more than determination to succeed in the business of risk management. Darko now knows that competence, conscience and confidence are more helpful traits than determination.

Both men confer that their moods about the insurance business have been lifted over the past few days.

"Thanks again Ned, our ride to and from the conference was definitely enlightening. Please shower us again with your wisdom and insight," Darko says bristling with his newfound enthusiasm.

"Before we get started, I would like to report that I already met with John in person and I wrote his auto, home and umbrella coverage. He accepted all of my advice and I set a follow up appointment to discuss his health insurance and his life insurance. I am now ready to roll," Tony says.

"Excellent," Ned says, "and thanks for the praise. I will start our exercise by discussing our itinerary. In the first part of our discussion, I will explain to you my philosophy regarding health insurance. We will revisit health maintenance organizations (HMO's) and preferred provider organizations (PPO's). We will then discuss health savings accounts (HSA's) and high-deductible plans. Finally, we will cover some of the new regulations and benefits associated with the Affordable Care Act (ACA). Based on this information, I will teach you how to implement the insurance buying strategy into your clients' health insurance purchases.

"Remember, your clients' health insurance will be a significant place for you to earn their trust and respect, as most of your clients will be in dire need of some competent advice in this critical component of their insurance portfolio. After completion of this discussion, Tony and I will continue with the role-play, and we will prepare him for his upcoming appointment with his friend and new client," Ned says.

"Sounds like a good plan to me," Darko says.

"I'm all ears," Tony agrees.

"Remember, your efforts will be 90 percent preparation and 10 percent presentation. In my case, I have spent considerably more time reading and learning than I have spent conducting comprehensive insurance presentations. You need to understand the products that you sell, and you must always be on the cutting edge of product innovation, adaptation and enhancement.

"Ben Franklin told us long ago, an ounce of prevention is worth more than a pound of cure. If you are not prepared and do not possess a firm belief, your clients will sense this and may hold you accountable. Your preparation and education will allow you to conduct your presentations in less time and with greater effectiveness.

"When you are prepared and have a defined purpose, you will be confident in your delivery and you'll find that people will buy your confidence more often than not," he impresses. "Your confidence will allow them to make confident buying decisions, so your convictions, in effect, will bring reduced anxiety to the process for both parties.

"All right, allow me to educate and prepare you on the subject of health insurance," Ned opens. "I am not being presumptuous when I say that health insurance can have life and death consequences."

"I don't understand what you mean by life or death consequences," Tony admits. "Please explain."

"Your question leads us back to the discussion of HMO's and PPO's," Ned begins. "First of all, I want my clients to receive universal access to medical providers. I want my clients to be able to seek the care they will need in the event of a significant health crisis. If my client needs access to the finest doctors and hospital facilities in the country in order to save their life or the life of a family member, I feel it is my duty to provide them with this type of insurance.

"For these reasons, I advise my clients to purchase PPO's with a strong national provider network. In addition, I will only write plans that allow my clients to access providers outside of their network, albeit for a reduced benefit. My firm belief in universal access has been fortified by some significant claims I have seen. I've seen how universal access has eliminated potential life and death consequences. I do not want to die waiting in a line for medical attention and I am certain my clients don't either," Ned explains.

"Can you give us some examples?" Tony asks.

"No Tony, I am going to make you research this on your own," Ned says.

"Well, can you tell me where I need to research this?" Tony asks again.

"I am kidding again, Tony," Ned chides. "I admire both your optimism and your enthusiasm. Of course I will give you some real life cases.

"One of my clients suffered a serious knee injury, and after surgery there were complications," he starts. "This led to multiple surgeries, which only seemed to worsen his situation. Eventually, two very distinguished university hospitals recommended amputation. Obviously, this was a very disconcerting prognosis. My client, out of desperation, researched his condition and found hope at the Mayo Clinic. Their prognosis was far more optimistic, and they assured my client that they could possibly save his leg.

"In the end, the doctors were able to save my client from a devastating amputation. My client is still able to lead a very active lifestyle. I believe that because he had a PPO and the ability to choose his own provider, he experienced a miraculous recovery," Ned pauses and then continues with another situation where universal access played a significant role in one of his clients' lives.

"In another case, a client of mine was in dire need of a liver transplant. Approaching death, my client was saved by a live donor transplant. My client's sister donated a portion of her liver in order to save the life of her brother. He has made a full recovery and is back to work and play. During his illness, he traveled the country searching for a cure and found one at a prestigious university hospital," Ned stops.

"So you believe if either client had had an HMO, they would have suffered a different fate?" Darko asks.

"I can't answer that question for certain," Ned responds, "however, I will say that I would never buy an HMO for myself.

"Our agency helped both of these clients through their trying times. I learned that I don't want to risk being caught in a bureaucratic shuffle at the risk of my own health; therefore, I will not provide HMO coverage for my clients. I believe the alternatives are more prudent.

"Once again, my agency will stay on the cutting edge of product innovation, adaptation and enhancement and will always respond to market change," he imparts his firm belief.

"I believe my brother has an HMO, so we will be having a discussion really soon," Tony says.

"If my clients have coverage at their work and they choose an HMO when they have the option of choosing a PPO, I must implore them to take the PPO option because it provides a lower out-of-pocket cost," Ned says.

"If you asked my clients what their out-of-pocket costs were for their harrowing medical experiences, I doubt any of them could accurately recall. The out-of-pocket expenditures were inconsequential to them, and thus meaningless. Their concerns were, 'will my leg be saved', and 'will my life be saved,'" Ned finishes.

"This is simple enough to understand," Darko says. "All insurance is about perils and consequences."

"You forgot about truths and realities," Tony adds.

"I didn't forget, but those two stories were all about perils and consequences," Darko responds.

"I am encouraged by both of your convictions," Ned says. "My goal is to make your convictions the fabric of your existence, and I am starting to observe significant results."

"Please continue," Darko directs. "I promise to sell only PPO's."

"Excellent, our next exercise will be to choose a plan design for our clients. With the advent of the health savings account (HSA) and some of the high deductible options, there is almost no case where I recommend anything else."

"My understanding is that HSA designs do not offer prescription drug coverage," Darko says. "Doesn't this create problems for your clients?"

"In most cases, prescription drug costs will be a relatively minor expense," Ned explains. "With the significant premium savings your clients will receive, the HSA, with a high deductible plan, will be most of your clients' best long-term purchase.

"I have not found a case where the math does not work in the client's favor. Once again, insurance is a logical arithmetic problem. As in a math problem, an insurance problem also has a logical undeniable solution," he says.

"I seem to get resistance on the drug prescription plan and higher deductible," Darko comments.

"Your resistance comes from the fact that you are not sitting your clients down and solving their insurance problem with a logical mathematical solution," Ned suggests.

"Remember, you must consider all insurance purchases from a long-term perspective. If a client has a claim soon after implementing an insurance buying strategy, the strategy may not work in the short term, which is a risk. The short-term risk is always inconsequential. Here are some examples: let's create a logical mathematical solution for Tony's friend and client before we begin our role-play," he says.

"At your request, I have the information regarding the health insurance for John's wife and children," Tony says as he hands the information to Ned.

"How old are they?" Ned asks.

"John is 37 years old, his wife Lisa is 34, and their children are eight and six years old," Tony says.

"And remind us of their current insurance plan," Ned says.

"They pay a premium of $1,300 per month, with a PPO plan with zero deductible and $12,500 out-of-pocket maximum."

"In that case," Ned starts, "I will recommend they purchase an HSA compatible plan with a $10,000 deductible and a $12,500 annual out-of-pocket maximum. They can then apply their premium savings in a health savings account. Those premium savings are tax-deductible. With the Affordable Care Act, if their income is below $95,400, they can receive subsidies for their monthly premiums."

"How much will the HSA plan cost on a monthly basis?" Tony asks.

"The premium for the health savings account compatible plan will be $868 per month. They will save nearly $440 per month," Ned answers. "However, because of the Affordable Care Act (ACA), John and Lisa can apply up to $6,650 per year, tax-free, in an HSA. If they do this, it will reduce their income from $100,000 to $93,350. This will put them below the $95,400-income level, which will allow them to get premium assistance of $295 per month. Their net monthly premium will then be $563.

"This means that, with this HSA plan, they will be saving $737 compared to their old plan."

"They must be giving up quite a lot to save that much premium," Darko says.

"They will only be assuming risk for inconsequential events," Ned says. "Let's start our role-play now, and this exercise will answer all of your questions."

"I hope you'll be able to perform magic on my health insurance," Tony starts, "because as I said before, the premiums are substantial."

"I never perform magic," Ned says, "but I will be able to improve your health insurance buying conditions.

"I will recommend that you purchase an HSA compatible plan," Ned says, "and the monthly premium will be $563. You are currently playing $1,300 per month. This will result in a $737 a month savings which translates into an $8,844 annual savings."

"I must be giving up something to garner such savings," Tony contributes.

"In the short-term, you may give up something, however in the long term you'll improve your health insurance buying strategy beyond reproach," Ned responds.

"Your current coverage provides you with a zero deductible per person and a zero family deductible. After meeting your deductibles, though, you will still be responsible for 20 percent of all expenses up to $6,250 per person and $12,500 for your entire family," he says.

"The low deductible is misleading, because after my deductible I am responsible for an additional $6,250," Tony says.

"Exactly," Ned says. "Your total out-of-pocket exposure is $6,250 for one person or $12,500 for your entire family. The HSA has a $10,000 annual deductible and a maximum annual out-of-pocket of $12,500 for your family."

"A $10,000 deductible is a lot of upfront money," Tony comments. "I don't think I like that."

"With the HSA approach your deductible is inconsequential to the strategy, since the premium savings is so significant," Ned says. "Once again, you will save $8,844 in annual premiums. My advice would be to purchase the health savings account compatible plan for $563 a month and save $737 a month. You will then be able to contribute some of the savings to a health savings account.

"For example, if you were to save $737 a month in a health savings account, at the end of three years you would have $26,532 saved. This would be more than enough to take care of your annual deductible. The longer you go without significant claims, the more money you will save. Long-term you cannot go wrong using this strategy. A health savings account will be the best way for you and your family to purchase their health insurance," he impresses.

"To be honest, it seems too good to be true," Tony adds.

"There is no difference between the inadequate coverage you have on your home and autos and the inadequate health insurance you currently have for your family," Ned clarifies.

"I told you at the outset that most of the people I meet with will be over-insured where coverage is least needed and under-insured where coverage is most needed. Your entire insurance portfolio has fulfilled this promise. For instance, you were grossly under-insured on your home, your liability insurance, and your uninsured motorist coverage. Your health insurance has you grossly over-insured where your coverage is least needed, too.

"You see the real problem that you face is that no one has explained this to you. It is obvious you have never had your insurance examined as one single product. The agent who added your family to your health insurance plan didn't care that you had other options. He or she made the decision that it was not worth their time to explain this void in strategy.

"For the first time, you'll have an insurance portfolio that is in your best interest, because for the first time, you will have examined your insurance risks as one financial product, with one advisor, and one solution," Ned reiterates, paraphrasing his declaration of intent.

"Do you have to contribute to the health savings account?" Tony asks.

"No you do not have to contribute to the health savings account," Ned answers. "In fact, the HSA compatible plan remains the best available option for you even if you decide not to make contributions. However, I would advise you make at least $400 monthly contribution to take advantage of the subsidies provided by the ACA."

"Great, how do I get started?" Tony asks.

"We will have to complete an application and then submit it to the insurance company," Ned says. "Within 30 to 60 days, they will either accept or reject your application. Based on your family's excellent health history, I anticipate an acceptance.

"In the meantime, you must continue with your current group insurance coverage. Upon your acceptance, I will then advise you to cancel your existing coverage."

"Fantastic," Tony affirms, "I am ready to roll."

"Great," Ned continues. "Our next step will be to discuss your most critical insurance coverage of all, which is your life insurance."

"With all of the savings you created with the new health insurance plan, I guess I will be able to afford life insurance, after all," Tony says.

"Based on your current financial condition, you can't afford not to have life insurance," Ned responds.

"Life insurance!" Darko interjects. "You are going to show me how to finally make my manager happy."

"Darko this is not about your manager's happiness," Ned reminds him. "It is all about your clients' financial security."

The health insurance discussion was yet another eye-opener for the eager and committed students. The importance of an insurance buying strategy has been illustrated to perfection. Darko and Tony learned that the health savings account was more than a strategy, and would, in fact, be mandatory for most of their clients. Ned's logical and ethical stand is beginning to dominate their thinking as they roll into the life insurance discussion.

Chapter 11 Summary

- Your clients' health insurance will be a significant place for you to earn their trust and respect, as most of your clients will be in dire need of some competent advice.
- Your clients should receive universal access to medical providers:
  - They should be able to seek the care they will need in the event of a significant health crisis.
  - They need access to the finest doctors and hospital facilities in the country in order to save their life or the life of a family member,
  - You should advise your clients to purchase a PPO with a strong national provider network. In addition, only write plans that allow your clients to see providers outside of their network, albeit for a reduced benefit.
- With the significant premium savings your clients will receive, the health savings account (HSA) with a high deductible plan will be your clients' best long-term purchase.
  - Your client does not have to contribute to the health savings account.
  - The HSA compatible plan remains the best available option even if they decide not to make contributions.
  - The plan design by itself is a distinct advantage over their existing plan design.
  - You should advise them to make monthly contributions so they will be prepared in the event of a significant claim. These contributions may be tax-deductible.
  - Because of the subsidies provided as part of the Affordable Care Act, sometimes making significant contributions can reduce your clients' annual income to levels sufficient for them to receive subsidies for their monthly payments.
- You will have to complete an application and then submit it to the insurance company. Within 30 to 60 days, they will either accept or reject the application, and you can contact your client to set up their coverage.

CHAPTER 12

THE ULTIMATE CONSEQUENCE INTERVIEW PART IV

"I realize Darko that you want to jump right back into the role-play," Ned says, "however, I first want to discuss why life insurance is oftentimes the most consequential of all Insurance coverage.

"For John and Lisa, their current life insurance program is their most glaring gap in coverage," he starts. "Tony was able to close the gaps on their casualty insurance by providing them with an undeniable alternative to their previous inadequate representation.

"People need to buy life insurance for the sole and express purpose of providing their loved ones with the loss of income their family will suffer upon their untimely death. In addition, life insurance can be structured to provide supplemental retirement savings and income.

"Life insurance provides survivors with the money they will need in order to continue the fulfillment of their hopes, their dreams, and their aspirations. Life insurance will not bring back lost loved ones, but life insurance *will* secure a family's continued success. Nearly all parents who I meet with are very concerned about their children's future and they realize money will be very important to its success.

"John and Lisa want and need life insurance, because they love their family," he continues, "and in the end, it will be Tony's responsibility to provide them with the proper and suitable solution to fulfill their hopes, their dreams, and their aspirations. Tony will be able to accomplish this by making himself accountable to their entire family," Ned imparts.

"Sometimes people just don't get it," Tony says.

"People don't get it because their insurance agent doesn't get it," Ned says. "A trusted insurance advisor is able to provide their clients with the proper life insurance because they believe in life insurance, and they are able to explain it to their clients in a clear and concise manner.

"Trusted insurance advisors do not sell insurance for the commissions they receive. Trusted insurance advisors sell life insurance for the coverage it provides families in times of need. Trusted insurance advisors realize providing life insurance is the right thing to do because they act through their conscience and not through their ego," Ned impresses.

"All right, I understand. I will not sell life insurance for anybody except the client," Darko contributes.

"Good," Ned says. "Then we will move on to determine the proper and suitable life insurance program that John, Lisa, and their children will need to satisfy their loss of income exposure.

"Earlier I indicated that a suitable amount of insurance to replace a wage earner's income with dependents would be approximately 10 times their annual income. John indicated through Tony that he had one year's salary for life insurance benefits through his job. If John were to die tomorrow, Lisa would receive $75,000, and then she would receive monthly benefits from Social Security."

"How much would they receive from Social Security?" Tony asks.

"I was prepared for that question," Ned responds, "and the answer is $3,400 a month until the second child reaches the age of 18.

"I determined that by going onto the Social Security administration's website and plugging in John's income and age. Here are the results," he says, displaying them on his computer.

(The link to the online calculator to determine Social Security benefits for survivors is http://www.ssa.gov/OACT/quickcalc/index.html).

"That is really easy to determine," Tony says. "I didn't realize that that information was at your fingertips."

"The information age has brought nearly all information to our fingertips," Ned says. "Remember, you must prepare and educate yourself, and part of your education is to be able to navigate the internet for critical information such as Social Security survivor benefits. Life is 90 percent preparation and 10 percent presentation.

"John's income is $75,000 a year and they would be left with one year's salary, plus an additional $3,400 a month from Social Security survivor benefits. The only way to make up the lost income would be through life insurance or through a radical change in their lifestyle. I don't believe Tony wishes to be a partner in a radical change in any family's lifestyle. Is that true Tony? " Ned asks the junior devotee.

"Absolutely not," Tony answers. "I promise to hold myself accountable. John and Lisa will buy life insurance because it is very clear that they need it."

"Excellent," Ned says. "The nominal insurance Tony has at work is inconsequential. He has the potential of losing this insurance, so I would just consider it a bonus and I will not factor this coverage into their total need. Tony will need a minimum of $750,000 of insurance or 10 times his income. Seven hundred and fifty thousand dollars will generate $37,500 of income assuming a five percent return on his investment with no capital depletion. The family will receive $40,800 a year from their Social Security survivor benefits, so a $750,000 policy coupled with their Social Security benefits will adequately replace their lost income."

"Do you always advise people to purchase 10 times their annual income for their life insurance benefit?" Tony asks.

"If their survivors are dependent upon their income, then the 10 times factor is most often adequate protection," Ned responds. "You will need to do the math for each client, and in some cases, you will find some people will need less than 10 times of their annual income and some people will need more.

"For instance, you may have a client who may have some exorbitant short-term debt or may be involved in a business deal that will require more coverage to satisfy their dependents' needs. These instances will be less common, but you must be prepared to provide a suitable solution," he says.

"You have made repeated references that life insurance and loss of income are most of your clients' greatest risk," Darko notices aloud. "Would you please explain this further?"

"Certainly," Ned says, "let's take John and Lisa and their financial situation.

"We determined before that their liability exposure was $650,000. We just determined that John's life insurance need was $750,000. Let's assume John was involved in an at fault accident, where severe bodily injury or a fatality occurred to another party. Let's also assume that this accident occurred prior to Tony's insurance intervention. John and Lisa would have been responsible for their additional exposure. Let's assume that the exposure was $300,000. John and Lisa would have been able to overcome this loss over a period of time, by paying for it out of their own pocket. This would cause them financial hardship, but would not lead to financial ruin.

"If John were to die prior to Tony's insurance intervention, this would lead the family to financial ruin as John's income would be vanquished forever. Without considering inflation or promotions, John's lost income over the next 25 years would be $1,875,000. The family would receive $489,600 in Social Security survivor benefits over the next 12 years, leaving the family with a total of $1,385,400 in lost income. In this case, the loss of income is his family's greatest financial exposure.

"Lost income due to a death is unrecoverable. I realize many things can happen that could offset this loss of income. Lisa could remarry; she could become successful in a business endeavor; or she may get an inheritance. Why, though, take the risk when there is an affordable solution? Why would you put your family's financial future in such peril?" Ned questions.

"Thank you for the clear and concise answer," Darko says. "How much coverage would you recommend for Lisa?"

"I would advise $300,000 life insurance for Lisa," Ned answers. "She earns $25,000 a year and, in addition, cares for the children. A $300,000 term policy is very inexpensive for a healthy 34-year-old."

"You would recommend term insurance for both of them?" Tony asks.

"Yes, I would," Ned responds. "I am more concerned with replacing income to the full extent. I feel at this point, they should be more concerned with their income replacement than the savings they would realize by starting a universal life policy or a variable universal life policy. If they were maximizing all of their retirement options, I may advise them to purchase a variable universal life product for a portion of their coverage to supplement their retirement.

"My guess is that Tony will find this is not the case for John and Lisa. You must be careful when you advise people to buy permanent life insurance products. In fact, I believe many agents will underinsure the risk in order to finance a permanent insurance product. I am most concerned with providing my clients with the deep pockets that life insurance will provide. I am most concerned with the children and spouses being able to fulfill their hopes, dreams and aspirations. Most term insurance policies are convertible to permanent insurance products, so you have the flexibility to revisit this at a later time. The truth is that most people are not taking full advantage of their 401(k) s, IRA's, or other retirement options," he says.

"That goes against conventional insurance wisdom, doesn't it?" Darko asks.

"I don't believe it goes against conventional insurance wisdom at all," Ned says. "Term insurance product conditions have improved significantly over time. In order for John to properly fund $750,000 of permanent insurance, the cost would be approximately $500 a month. Five hundred dollars a month would represent more than five percent of the family's monthly income. Tony would have a tough time convincing John and Lisa of the value and would perhaps jeopardize the acquisition of the account. John and Lisa would then continue to be grossly under-insured or would go somewhere else to purchase the adequate term life insurance that they need.

"Permanent insurance is designed more for estate cases or for high income earners who are already maximizing all of their retirement options. My position is to provide protection for the loss of income risk, first and foremost," he finishes.

"What about the cost of waiting?" Darko asks.

"The cost of being under-insured is of greater consequence than the cost of waiting," Ned says. "I believe the true cost of waiting comes from waiting so long to buy life insurance that you become uninsurable.

"John and Lisa are still young and healthy, and therefore, insurable. As time passes, people become less and less insurable. John or Lisa may develop a cholesterol problem, diabetes, or a myriad of other conditions that can affect their insurability.

"Tony's job will be to provide them with a significant offer from a life insurance company. John and Lisa will need at least 20 years of level term insurance and they will need to be healthy enough to warrant an offer from a carrier. As people age, they do not get healthier, so Tony must qualify them as soon as possible. Insurability is the true cost of waiting; therefore, my advice is to adequately insure their risk from the outset. You want to make certain that there are convertibility privileges on all of the term policies you write. Convertibility is paramount," Ned stops.

"We have a game plan, so let's resume our role-play," Darko suggests.

"Are you ready Tony?" Ned asks.

"I am," Tony responds.

"Upon your untimely death, you want to be certain that your family will be able to continue living the same lifestyle. Is this correct?" Ned asks.

"Yes, I would like for my wife and children to be able to continue to go forward financially," Tony says, as John. "I don't want them to have to sell the house or alter their lifestyle in any way."

"Excellent," Ned says, "we first must determine the amount of coverage you'll need in order to meet your goals. Based on your current income, the Social Security administration will provide your wife with $3,400 a month in survivor benefits until your second child reaches the age of 18. This leaves approximately a $2,850 per month gap in income that they will need in order to replace your income," Ned pauses.

"How much insurance will it take to generate $2,850 in income?" Tony asks.

"I will advise you to purchase a 20-year term insurance policy for $750,000 in coverage," Ned begins. "Assuming a conservative 5 percent return, $750,000 will produce $37,500 a year or $3,125 per month in income. I will advise you to purchase a 20-year term insurance policy for your wife, with coverage in the amount of $300,000.

"The monthly premium for your policy could range from as low as $60 a month to as high as $150 a month. Your wife's premium could range from as low as $20 a month to as high as $50 a month. You will both be required to take a physical in order to secure the coverage. The results of the physical will determine the cost of your policies. The company has the right to reject your coverage based on adverse medical information," he explains.

"What type of physical do they give me?" Tony asks.

"You'll have all of your vitals taken," Ned says. "They will test your blood-pressure and heart rate, and they will also take a blood and urine sample. The insurance company will pay for the bill, so you can view it as a free physical."

"I'd like to think about it, talk it over with my wife, and research it a little bit. How does that sound?" Tony asks.

"The application process can take between 30 and 60 days," Ned says. "That will give you plenty of time to think about it, and frankly, I have already done your research. I will advise you to complete the application, and set up the physical. By overhauling your entire insurance portfolio, we have reduced your overall costs to the point that, even with the life insurance, you will be paying less than you were before. Let's face it, you and your family really need this coverage since it is critical to your financial well-being."

"You're right," Tony says, "so how do we get started?"

"I will need to collect a check for the first month's premium," Ned says. "I will estimate the premium for both policies to be $115 a month. As I said before, the insurance companies offering them may come back with a lower or a higher premium. Once they make their offer, we will meet again to place the coverage."

"Wait a second," Darko interjects, "those were soft objections. 'I'd like to think about it. You're right, so how do we get started.'"

"Darko, those objections were about as bold as they come," Ned says. "From start to finish, the declaration of intent overhauled John and Lisa's entire insurance portfolio. Their previous insurance portfolio was a complete mess. Like nearly all the people in the marketplace, they were grossly under-insured in many critical areas, and they had absolutely no strategy.

"The entire interview process makes it clear that insurance is the financial foundation, and you must view it as *one single product, with one advisor, and one solution*.

"You see, Darko, there is no closing in this interview, because insurance is too important of a product to close. People close car deals and real estate deals. You don't close insurance buying strategies. You provide them. I promise you it works like this every single time. People want cars, people want real estate, but people need insurance. People need auto, home, umbrella, health and life insurance. I promise you, Darko, you will no longer have to close deals if you follow the tenets and principles of my mission statement and declaration of intent. It won't happen overnight, but if you are diligent and disciplined, it will happen. I know this because it has happened to me and to all of my associates.

Ned has completed the comprehensive insurance review for Tony's friend, John, but his devotees sense that there is one more lesson in store for them. They both sit quietly in anticipation of Ned's discussion of their greatest opportunity.

Chapter 12 Summary

- People need to buy life insurance for the sole and express purpose of providing their loved ones with the loss of income their family will suffer upon their untimely death.
- Life insurance provides survivors with the money they will need in order to continue the fulfillment of their hopes, their dreams, and their aspirations.
- A suitable amount of insurance to replace a wage earner's income with dependents would be approximately 10 times their annual income. This is in addition to whatever nominal life insurance coverage they have through their employer and the minimal benefits Social Security will provide.
- You should recommend term life insurance to your clients and make sure it is convertible into a permanent product like variable or universal life. Also, make sure the level term extends throughout the working lives of the couple.
- You should tell your clients that both spouses will be required to take a physical (paid for by the insurance agency) in order to secure the coverage. The results of the physical will determine the cost of their policies. The company has the right to reject their coverage based on adverse medical information.
- Estimate the premium and collect a check before you submit the life application and before they take their physical. The actual premium could either be higher or lower, but it is important to get the application process started, which can take up to 60 days.

"Without the strength to endure the crisis, one will not see the opportunity within. It is within the process of endurance that opportunity reveals itself."

- Chin-Ning Chu

THE GREATEST OPPORTUNITY

"I must admit that I am very confident in my beliefs, and I know the principles I follow have been tested over time. The results of applying my beliefs have borne true, so please, allow me to share your greatest opportunity," Ned begins.

"Understanding, from what you have taught, that we must become master communicators of our principles and beliefs through our verbal communication, we look forward to one final rant," Darko directs.

Ned begins, "The four perils—property peril, lawsuit peril, medical insurance peril, and the loss of income peril—cannot be avoided. You cannot stop fire; illnesses may loom; litigation may threaten; disability and mortality will happen. These occurrences are all unavoidable, and in fact they happen every day.

"I believe your greatest opportunity is the existence of a final fifth peril," Ned says, before Darko interrupts.

"Wait," he says in disbelief, "you're telling me there are FIVE perils, not four?"

"Yes, Darko, but as I was saying, the fifth peril holds your greatest opportunity, and the beauty of this peril is that it is the only peril that can be avoided. It is the peril of inadequate representation and it can be eradicated through competence and integrity.

"Competent representation comes from acting as an advisor, building insurance buying strategies, and, at the same time, recognizing the existence of the four perils so you can act in the best interest of the client. Adhering to the consequential and inconsequential coverage philosophy, while diagnosing all transactions in person, unlocks the tall gates and is the key to exposing the inadequacies of competition.

"It has been my goal, through all of these talks, to help both of you to follow logical, rational principles in order to gain an indomitable advantage over your competitors. We do this, and gain confidence during the process, through continuous education and an impregnable commitment to our clients. It is imperative to keep a beginner's mind to be open to new products, approaches and ideas that may significantly help your clients," he finishes.

Darko's eyes light up as he realizes the direction Ned's conversation is taking. He smiles and delivers a heartfelt contribution to the discussion.

"I have come to understand through all of our discussions that from a place of both knowledge and commitment we are able to find our voice," he says. "That vision and declaration of intent helps our clients understand insurance as a single financial product. All of this combined makes me understand how the fifth peril is my greatest advantage."

"Excellent response Darko," Ned praises. "The declaration of intent is the vision leading to deeper understanding and a personal voice. The vision is guided by our commitment to the client and allows us to avoid the perils associated with inadequate representation. You must know what you're doing, and then you must be able to explain it to your clients and put them at ease."

"If you have a defined mission and purpose, you won't have to sell anymore, will you?" Tony queries.

"Precisely, Tony," Ned says.

"Transparency forces agents to become more ethical," Tony adds.

"I believe most agents want to be ethical," Ned clarifies. "The problem is they are taught how to sell insurance. Selling insurance leads you to unethical practice. On the other hand, ethical insurance practice provides your clients with a suitable and logical insurance buying strategy based upon sound principles that enable the client to transfer all of their consequential risk.

"Rather than focusing on integrity and vision, the industry has tended to emphasize rules and procedures, marketing techniques, sales pitches, and systems.

"You see, our clients are blind to the perils they face, and it is the responsibility of an advisor to lead their clients down a path to safety. The days of selling insurance are coming to an end because it is not logical or fair for the blind to lead the blind. People will say that life is not always fair, but each individual has the power and choice to be fair.

"To me, it is very simple. You must realize that you have to advise people when they are entering into legal contracts that allow them to transfer risk. This is a very serious business. Selling and using sales techniques are things of the past," Ned finishes.

"Ned, as I have been listening to you, I have begun to think about all the people in my own life and how I would like for them to be advised and protected against threats that could take away the life they now know," Tony adds.

"Realizing this made me ask myself why, if I want that for my own family, I am not providing this security to my clients. I would have to say that is your greatest lesson. My clients need me to treat them as if they were my mother, father, son, or daughter. You have taught me that I must put my clients' interests ahead of mine at all times."

"You're exactly right, Tony," Ned says. "You must treat your clients as if they were your own family. Isn't it true that the human race is one family? Isn't it true that, as a culture, we lose sight of this far too often? When you take this opportunity to treat your clients like your own family, then your career and life will flourish."

Darko, with understanding dawning within him like the Eastern sun, jumps in.

"When you put it that way, it made me realize that my family has better coverage than my clients do. My clients don't have the proper coverage because I have been selling them insurance, lacking in forthrightness and conviction. With my family I put aside ego and have one sole purpose, to protect them. I have realized in those settings that

I have put aside the pursuit of money for the security of those I care about. That has made my purpose significant, and with that guiding vision I am able to place them with the needed coverage. This time with you, Ned, has convinced me that I must take that same ethical stance with my clients.

"Darko, I believe you've got it," Ned says. "Your skepticism arose from allowing your ego to supersede your conscience. When people act on their own behalf most of the time, their personal development is always impeded."

"I have found that following your conscience will take more time in the beginning," Tony starts, "but in the end the results will be more gratifying, and as you said, more meaningful."

"It is a beautiful thing to imagine industries flourishing because they are operating through ethical practices and following their conscience," Ned says.

"Imagine your agency operating under the mission statement and the tenets and principles of my declaration of intent. Imagine your clients having ultimate trust in your competency and your expertise. Imagine your office as a team of associates living and breathing this vision. Imagine your entire agency implementing this vision."

Tony and Darko stare, wide-eyed, at the thought of this proposition.

"My agency has done just this," Ned continues. "The associates in my office have a wealth of knowledge that they are able to draw upon and evolve into a continuum with a life of its own. When I am gone, the vision continues without interruption. You see, I am not the business. The mission statement and declaration of intent are the business.

"Imagine leaving your office for six weeks, and coming back to no phone calls, no paperwork, and greater revenues. Imagine one of your agents being gone for two months with an illness and you still pay them and then they return to no phone calls, no paperwork and greater revenues. Imagine losing the urgency that dominates most business owners. Imagine losing the urgency to be there, to be the business, to be the rainmaker. Imagine clients being serviced by multiple advocates of the mission. Imagine clients, trusting the entire business, instead of select individuals within the organization."

Both Darko and Tony inhale deep, steadily and calmly.

Then, Darko, understanding the depth of possibilities contained within the mission and declaration of intent, confesses, "All along. I've been trying to find a faster more efficient way to sell more insurance and increase my revenues. You just made me realize that it's more important for me to be effective than it is to be efficient. I have always been efficient, but our discussion has exposed my lack of effectiveness and, as a result, freedom. If I implement the mission statement, along with the declaration of intent, into my business, then I must teach it to all of my staff and then everyone will be free."

"Exactly, Darko," Ned says, "you must teach this to everybody. You must perceive yourself as a mentor, a teacher and a leader. As such, you must look at those who work with you as people who have choices; you do not own them or their minds.

"This is very important, Darko, not only during the present moment but also because your future compensation will be derived from how you treat others. This compensation differs from monetary compensation because you can treat others poorly and still be handsomely compensated; however, this will never provide you with overall fulfillment.

"My teachings are about profiting on many levels. You will successfully increase revenues while, at the same time, exhaustively examine why it is you do what you do, giving your job as an advisor purpose. Even though the focus is not on the benefits that will come to you, and you are being asked to focus first on the interests of your clients, you will be rewarded.

"As you improve the lives of your clients, you will improve your life," Ned says.

"The mission statement and declaration of intent are my gifts to both you and the client. My hope is that you'll take this vision and give it to all those you encounter. I believe this has the power to change not only the reputation of the industry, but also the industry itself.

"I believe this because my own time and experience has taught me the effect of creating a doctrine of absolute trust in a world that profits mostly through distrust. By making trustworthiness commonplace, we elevate ourselves above industries in which distrust is pervasive."

"Well, I guess I'm glad that most people don't have the right insurance today, because if they did, then I wouldn't have this great opportunity before me," Darko comments.

"If trustworthiness was commonplace already, I would be left with no opportunity," Tony says.

Ned studies both men attempting to step back into their world. He understands that they have not yet experienced the effect of good begetting good and the exponential way it profits everyone involved.

"That is not true, Tony," he begins. "If trustworthiness were commonplace, your opportunities would be unlimited.

"Imagine a company taking this mission and declaration of intent and making it a curriculum for all those in the organization. Imagine all executives following these directives. Imagine claims adjusters and underwriters engaged in this philosophy. Imagine a company shedding the rules and procedures to follow these principles. Imagine an entire company operating under this philosophy. Imagine an end to the bureaucracy, cheating and manipulation that challenge most industries.

"The public will pay for services, regardless of the price, provided by such trustworthy industries because they will perceive an enormous value to themselves. They will be receiving an enormous value in the form of peace of mind.

"The insurance industry offers to provide the public with an equitable transfer of their insurmountable risk, nothing less and nothing more, and clients will trust that this is exactly what is being done," Ned says.

"Remember, following principles allows you to achieve a greater understanding of your discipline than following rules and regulations," he continues. "You are more adaptive to change when you follow principles, and where there is change, there is opportunity.

"In order to grow and move into the future, our profession needs the declaration of intent. Change is inevitable. In order to be prepared for it, our profession must adopt this mission based on principle so that it will no longer helplessly react to the continuous change, but instead, seamlessly facilitate it.

"The declaration of intent allows our profession to seek out greater opportunities and respond to the ever-changing landscape. The declaration of intent is a reasonable and logical approach that benefits all parties. It creates a win-win-win situation.

"First, the insurance company wins because its advisors are suitably and equitably transferring their clients' risk. As a result, the company reduces exposure to bad faith and incompetence, and customers will have more satisfaction when a major claim occurs. It is then, especially, that they will realize the declaration of intent has provided them with the proper coverage in the event of all insurable worst-case scenarios.

"Second, small claim exposures that have gobbled profits are eliminated and transferred to the clients who must assume a greater amount of low-end risk.

"Next, the declaration convinces consumers that their insurance is not a necessary evil or a financial drain, but an essential part of their financial well-being. In turn the company wins because the advisor took care of the claim before the claim happened.

"Everyone wins when the entire industry engages in continuous adherence to truth and the reality that there are perils and consequences."

All men nod their heads in agreement, considering the way everyone benefits from the vision of the declaration of intent. Not only does it bring dignity to the client and the advisor, but also to the industry. They all become pensive thinking about the impact such integrity can have for all of those involved. As they venture on this mental path, Ned echoes all of their thoughts.

"Imagine this mission and vision spreading from us, one by one, to an entire company and then to an entire industry. Imagine taking this philosophy and sharing it with your associates and working for a company that embraces the philosophy of commitment. Imagine providing the curriculum of this philosophy to all in the organization and the exponential effect of that commitment. Might the company who adopts this philosophy transcend itself to true market leadership? Might it change the way the game is played? I believe so. But it all begins here with us and our willingness to share what we are learning with others," Ned continues.

"Just the mere sharing of knowledge will break down the walls of mistrust plaguing our profession. A positive public perception, through an infusion of competence and integrity, will proliferate through our clients. No longer will consumers be bombarded with confusing, fear-inspiring, insurance marketing strategies. Instead, they will receive promises that are kept," Ned's eyes are slightly glazed as he continues to think about the impact of positive business practices. The benefits of leading an ethical life seem endless.

"We have the capability of becoming pioneers through the promotion of understanding. The clients themselves would become our very own marketing department and we would be able to live off of our reputations and direct referrals. Gone would be the time of spending money on endless commercials, ads and postcards.

"Marketing has contributed to the less than favorable public opinion about insurance because its emphasis is on numbers. Now, imagine an industry filled with professionals playing the people game, where all of their clients are treated as if they were family members, not like cardboard cutouts only to be talked to in hollowed out phrases and in slick pitches. Instead of offering worn out sales pitches, we should be people of action.

"Our industry needs to take direct action, and I believe this action will only come from the ground up. Insurance companies are too large and industrialized to make the change themselves. Real change will come from individuals and small, effective organizations demonstrating the efficiency, effectiveness and profitability of knowledge age workers. These are the ones who prove the workability of new ideas; they are the ones unafraid of change and small enough to begin redirection. Insurance companies have been reacting, instead of responding, to change for many decades.

"Our opportunity as advisors lies in this reality. We have the power to adapt to changing times and help our companies flourish in the knowledge age because, for the first time, we have choices and we can exercise our ability to think. For the first time, we can choose not to be things, mere cogs in the wheel, and, instead, clamor for reeducation and a change of direction, not on the basis of an impossible dream, but because it works.

"Instead of adhering to dried out rules and regulations we can insist on a change of focus. As our companies thrive, the industry will be forced to react to changing internal structures. Imagine, then, the public view of insurance agents who work for an industry that puts priority on the continual education of its employees in order for them to be the best they can be throughout their careers and provide the best and most trustworthy service. Agents would then be known for providing the proper insurance to their clients from the outset.

"I promise you, there are no secrets to success anymore. The days of professions benefiting from shrouds of mystery are coming to an end. The key to success is operating in such a fashion that a newfound transparency will reveal only knowledge, integrity, and the acknowledgement of reality.

"I have given you all the tools you'll need to carry out this declaration of intent. I know that it works and, most importantly, I know that it is right. My colleagues, associates and myself have proven it so," Ned completes his visionary speech.

Darko breaks the silence of truth to express his thanks to Ned.

"Your candor has awakened my spirit, and your declaration of intent has defined my new purpose. I will no longer work hopelessly for money, but I will now work to improve the lives of those who I encounter because I now know my freedom is dependent upon following your teachings and visions throughout the rest of my days," he says.

Tony shares Darko's sentiments and expresses his concern, "The only trepidation I have is how I will remember all that you have taught us. You should write it all down so I can reference the things I can't quite remember," Tony says.

Chapter 13 Summary

- Your greatest opportunity is the existence of a final fifth peril. It is the peril of inadequate representation and it can be eradicated through competence and integrity.
- Competent representation comes from acting as an advisor, building insurance buying strategies, and, at the same time, recognizing the existence of the four perils so you can act in the best interest of your client. Adhering to the consequential and inconsequential coverage philosophy, while diagnosing all transactions in person, is the key to exposing the inadequacies of competition.
- Your clients are blind to the perils they face, and it is the responsibility of an advisor to lead their clients down a path to safety.
- The declaration of intent is the fabric of your agency and it is followed each and every day. You are not the business. The declaration of intent is the business.
- Market leadership does not come from doing the same things your competitors do, but doing them better. Everyone wins when the entire industry engages in continuous adherence to truth and the reality that there are perils and consequences.
  - First, the insurance company wins because its advisors are suitably and equitably transferring their clients' risk. As a result, the company reduces exposure to bad faith and incompetence, and customers will have more satisfaction when a major claim occurs; it is then, especially, that they will realize the declaration of intent has provided them with the proper coverage in the event of all insurable worst-case scenarios.
  - Second, small claim exposures that have gobbled profits are eliminated and transferred to the clients who must assume a greater amount of low-end risk.

- ○ Next, the declaration convinces consumers that their insurance is not a necessary evil or a financial drain, but an essential part of their financial well-being. In turn, the company wins because the advisor took care of the claim before it happened.
- Take this wealth of knowledge and begin a new journey, a journey of hope and opportunity that is derived from adhering to universal principles that have been tested over time.

Acknowledgements

I would like to express my gratitude and appreciation to all of the people in my life including family, friends, clients, and business associates. Without your support and guidance throughout my life, this book would not have been possible.

I would like to thank all past and current employees and associates of my agency including Brett Binneweg, Tomika Clark, Breezy Child, Donna Spicer, my brother, Jeff Votaw, and of course, my wife, Susan Votaw.

I would like to thank Jon Ganea and the late Michael King who inspired and collaborated with me on thoughts and ideas. Thanks also to my business partner, Stan Scott, who helped me write and publish this book.

Thanks to Zonia Lucero, Maggie Thach, and Megan Brancaccio for their help editing the different versions of this book.

And finally, to my mentors, Ned Vukovich, Doug Dillard, and Ryan Nuttall, I have learned valuable insights from each of you that helped me in different ways throughout my career and in writing this book.

www.ingramcontent.com/pod-product-compliance
Lightning Source LLC
Chambersburg PA
CBHW030754180526
45163CB00003B/1026